EmBossed Imprints

A-Z of Leadership Traits

Sundararaman Ganapathiraman

INDIA • SINGAPORE • MALAYSIA

ISBN

Paperback : 979-8-89632-210-8
Hardcase : 979-8-89632-211-5

From the Author's Desk

Thank you for your purchase!

We hope this journey through "EmBossed Imprints: A-Z Leadership Traits" empowers and inspires you.

Checklist for Leadership Journey: *"EmBossed Imprints: A-Z Leadership Traits"*

Reader (Your) Information:

Name of Reader (Leader): ______________________

Current Designation: ______________________

Current Industry: ______________________

Years of Experience:

<10 years	10~20 years	20~30 years	>30 years

A-Z Traits Progress Tracker:

Tick each box as you complete your worksheet after each chapter:

A	B	C	D	E	F	G	H	I	J	K	L	M
N	O	P	Q	R	S	T	U	V	W	X	Y	Z

With best wishes for your leadership journey,

Sundararaman Ganapathiraman

Dedication

"I touch the future. I teach."

– Christa McAuliffe (American teacher, and astronaut who lost her life in the Challenger explosion in 1986)

We often believe that leadership qualities are inherent or emerge later in life. However, my experiences suggest that the seeds of leadership are often sown during our formative years. This book is dedicated to the inspiring educators who nurtured my growth during my formative years:

- Saiva Prakasa Vidyasala, Devakottai, Tamil Nadu (Primary School)
- E. R. Higher Secondary School, Trichy, Tamil Nadu
- REC Trichy (currently known as NIT Trichy), Tamil Nadu

Their guidance and support played a pivotal role in shaping my leadership skills and propelling me on a path of personal and professional development.

Contents

Cross Index of Leadership Traits and Leaders

A Note of Gratitude

"Other things may change us, but we start and end with the family."

– Anthony Brandt (American composer, academic, and writer)

This quote resonates deeply with me, and it's with immense gratitude that I dedicate this book to those who have been my unwavering support system:

- My dearest wife, Vijaya, for her unwavering love and encouragement.
- My twin daughters, Ramitha and Rochita, who fill my life with joy and inspire me to be a better person.
- My parents, close circle of relatives & friends, who have been a constant source of motivation and guidance on my professional journey.

Their belief in me has fuelled my passion and helped me reach new heights. This book wouldn't be possible without their love and support.

Foreword

by

Mr Vipin Sondhi

(Former MD & CEO Ashok Leyland, JCB India and Tecumseh India)

Mr. Vipin Sondhi

It is my great pleasure to be invited to write this Foreword by my esteemed colleague and friend, G. Sundararaman, as he shares his remarkable journey and insightful reflections on the exceptional individuals who have shaped his illustrious over 35-year career, which is incidentally still work-in-progress. He is the Co-CEO of Wipro-Pari. Sundar, as we have always called him, and I have had the privilege of sharing a significant part of our professional journey together, during an intense period for Indian Manufacturing, when it was transitioning in its quest for global quality and productivity. I first met him when he joined Tecumseh India (then Shriram Refrigeration Industries) and later our paths crossed again, happily for me, at JCB India.

Sundar's forte was Quality and Business Excellence. His knowledge, energy, dedication and passion for excellence in everything he did was always contagious to the entire organisation. What set him apart was his personal conviction and self-belief that Indian Manufacturing could aspire to compete with the best in the world. Both Tecumseh and JCB India grew over a period of time to be world-class, exporting compressors and construction equipment respectively around the world. During the latter part of his stint in JCB India, he first created a 'five man army' which grew into a 'One team One dream', of several hundred young, highly motivated, multi-function team of men and women from the grass-roots of Rajasthan, to build a first of its kind multi-product, greenfield world-class factory. From this plant emerged many firsts including the 'highly self-confident, best-in-class women welders of JCB'. Women who 'shattered stereo-types and displayed Strength' in Sundar's words. Each a champion in their own right.

EmBossed Imprints is a heartfelt tribute to the remarkable superiors, peers and subordinates who have influenced Sundar's career. Not many include the latter. But that is Sundar for you! Through a collection of poignant anecdotes, candid observations and valuable lessons, he weaves a narrative that celebrates the power of collaboration, mentorship and camaraderie to attain radically positive outcomes.

As you delve into these pages, you will encounter an array of exceptional individuals, each with their distinctive strengths, which Sundar has classified into A – Z of Leadership traits. You will meet visionary leaders who empowered and guided Sundar, talented peers who challenged and motivated him, and dedicated subordinates whose energy and potential he harnessed. Through their experiences, Sundar distils valuable insights on effective leadership, communication, teamwork, and personal growth.

What resonates throughout this book is Sundar's genuine admiration and gratitude for the people who have enriched his professional life. His writing is infused with humility and a deep appreciation for the human aspect of workplace relationships. He reminds us that, beyond organizational hierarchies, it is the people who make a difference; who shape our perspectives, foster our growth, and create lasting impact.

As someone who has had the privilege of witnessing Sundar's journey very closely, I can confidently say that this book is an authentic reflection of his character and values. His generosity in sharing these stories will undoubtedly inspire readers to reflect on their own professional relationships and strive for greater collaboration. And hopefully, start penning their own experiences down in a work-book style, that he has uniquely created.

In conclusion, I offer my warmest congratulations to Sundar, his lovely wife Vijaya and their brilliant twin daughters Ramitha and Rochita, on this outstanding treasure trove of heart-warming stories that will resonate with professionals across industries and levels. As you read these pages, I invite you to embrace the virtues and values that Sundar so eloquently celebrates; and to cultivate your own extraordinary network of relationships that will enrich your life and career.

I was fortunate to have worked with Sundar. And with so many of our colleagues.

Vipin Sondhi
(Former MD & CEO Ashok Leyland, JCB India and Tecumseh India)

Preface

"Be the leader you wish you had"

– Simon Sinek (English-born American author and speaker on business leadership)

Unleashing Your Inner Leader: My 35-year journey in the industrial world has been a rich tapestry of experiences. I've witnessed countless leaders, both inspiring and formidable. Through keen observation of my superiors and subordinates, I've gained valuable insights into the traits that make leaders truly successful.

This book is not just about leadership theory, it's about unlocking your own leadership potential. Packed with real-world anecdotes drawn from my experiences working with incredible people, these pages will serve as a guide to self-discovery.

Embrace the Power of Reflection: The book features 26 dedicated worksheets, each corresponding to a key leadership trait (A-Z). These worksheets are your personal leadership laboratory. As you encounter each trait, reflect on your own experiences. Jot down personal anecdotes that illustrate how you, a colleague, or a supervisor has embodied that trait.

Sharpen Your Leadership Lens: By actively engaging with these exercises, you'll cultivate a sharper eye for spotting leadership traits in everyday interactions. This newfound awareness empowers you to not only appreciate exceptional leadership but also emulate it in your own journey.

A Glimpse into the A-Z of Leadership: To give you a taste of what awaits, here's a list of the leadership traits explored in the book:

1. **A - Authentic:** Leads with genuine self-belief and transparency.
2. **B - Bold:** Takes calculated risks and seizes opportunities.
3. **C - Competitive:** Strives for excellence and motivates others to do the same.
4. **D - Driven:** Possesses a relentless pursuit of goals.
5. **E - Energized:** Infuses the team with enthusiasm and motivation.
6. **F - Fearless:** Makes tough decisions and isn't afraid of challenges.
7. **G - Grateful:** Appreciates contributions and fosters a positive environment.
8. **H - Honest:** Builds trust with open communication and integrity.
9. **I - Inspirational:** Motivates and empowers others to achieve their best.
10. **J - Just:** Makes fair decisions and treats everyone with respect.
11. **K - Knowledgeable:** Possesses expertise and fosters a culture of learning.
12. **L - Loyal:** Commands trust and dedication through unwavering support.
13. **M - Memorable:** Makes a lasting positive impact on those they lead.

14. **N - Networker:** Builds strong relationships and fosters collaboration.
15. **O - Obsessive:** Ensures accuracy and high standards.
16. **P - Persistent:** Never gives up and overcomes obstacles.
17. **Q - Qualified:** Possesses the skills and experience to lead effectively.
18. **R - Responsible:** Takes ownership of actions and decisions.
19. **S - Strong:** Demonstrates resilience, confidence, and decisiveness.
20. **T - Tactful:** Delivers feedback and navigates difficult situations with diplomacy.
21. **U - Unwavering:** Holds firm to their values and convictions.
22. **V - Visionary:** Sets a clear direction and inspires others to follow.
23. **W - Wary:** Exercises caution and considers all possibilities.
24. **X - Xeniel:** Embraces new ideas and perspectives.
25. **Y - Yearning:** Sets high goals and strives for continuous improvement.
26. **Z - Zealous:** Possesses a strong passion for the cause or vision.

(Source reference: https://www.inc.com/thomas-koulopoulos/the-alphabet-of-a-leader.html)

This book is an invitation to embark on a transformative journey. By harnessing the power of introspection and real-world examples, you can unlock your leadership potential and become the best leader you can be.

Throughout my career, I've had the privilege of working with exceptional leaders. I'm grateful for the mentorship of **Mr. S.S. Raman** (Whirlpool of India & TVS Electronics), **Mr. Vipin Sondhi** (Tecumseh India & JCB India)**, and Mr. Pratik Kumar** (Wipro Infrastructure). These experiences, spanning over three decades, have been periods of immense learning. **It is with deep honour and gratitude that I include Mr. Vipin Sondhi's foreword in this book.**

Introduction

"People who are truly strong, lift others up. People who are truly powerful bring others together."

– Michelle Obama (American attorney and author who served as the first lady of the United States)

Our professional growth is rarely a solo journey. By reflecting on significant moments, we can identify the leadership traits exhibited by those around us – bosses, peers, even subordinates – that played a crucial role in our success. This introspection fosters deeper understanding, appreciation, and stronger relationships in the workplace.

Personal Introduction:

Looking back on my own three-and-a-half-decade career, starting as a Graduate Engineer Trainee in 1989, I'm struck by the impact of numerous individuals. Leadership came in many forms, each unique and spontaneous. Early on, I experienced frequent leadership transitions – six bosses in the first decade alone. The pace slowed in the second decade with two, followed by a decade with one, and finally, the last five years with another.

Similarly, my team grew from none in the first two years to thousands as I led multi-function teams and factories across continents. Witnessing their growth over the years, I see many in senior leadership positions today, across various organizations worldwide. Each displayed exceptional strengths, emerging as capable leaders in their own right.

Thank you for choosing this book. Consider this an investment in your professional development. As you read, I invite you to reflect on pivotal moments in your own career. Identify the 26 leadership traits listed later and recall an anecdote where one was exemplified. Did you exhibit it? Your boss? A colleague? Depending on your career stage, you may or may not identify all 26 traits immediately, but whenever you identify use the workbook to record.

From My Anecdotes to Yours: A Shared Journey of Leadership:

Are you curious to discover the 26 leadership traits and how they played out in real-world scenarios? Perhaps you'll even recognize yourself or someone you know in these anecdotes. Let's embark on this journey of reflection together. Turn the page and get ready to unlock the leadership lessons hidden within your own professional life.

This book, "EmBossed Imprints," is not just a collection of my experiences, but a springboard for yours. As you delve into the different leadership styles explored throughout the A-Z of Leadership Traits, consider the anecdotes you'll inevitably encounter in your own career.

Fill the provided worksheets with these stories, identifying the traits exhibited and the individuals involved. By the end, you'll have a personalized record of your growth journey, enriched by the stories of those who helped you along the way.

Chapter 1

Bengaluru Baptism by Telex

Obsessive: Ensures accuracy and high standards

Trial by Telex

It was June 1989, a crisp Bengaluru morning just two weeks into my first real job as a Graduate Engineer Trainee (GET) at Sundram Fasteners Ltd.'s Vanivilas Road office. Fresh off a flight from Chennai, my fellow GET and I were wide-eyed newbies. My initiation wasn't at a computer terminal, but at a telex machine, learning the art of sending payment follow-up messages in morse code under the watchful eye of Kasthuri Rangan (who was my roommate as well). This was a ritual, we were told, instilled by **V.T.Govindarajan** (VTG), the then Marketing Manager.

VTG's Relentless Pursuit

VTG was a man of details. We had an outstanding customer payment of around Rs. 3 lakhs, overdue for over 90 days. He was relentless in his pursuit of every paisa owed. I vividly recall his frustration when I couldn't explain a measly Rs. 35 outstanding on a single bill.

Determined to collect, I embarked on an expedition to the customer's factory (MICO) in Adugodi. What followed was a bureaucratic odyssey. Guided by a finance officer, I was first sent to the stores department for an invoice copy, then on a wild goose chase to the inward QC department for a rejection note on a batch of parts with a dimensional discrepancy – a discrepancy that amounted to a debit of just Rs. 35 on our account! Back then, with no computers or ERPs, everything was manual and painfully slow.

Weeks later, armed with the rejection note, I was back at the factory, this time in Hosur. There, I was shuffled between the customer quality team, the final inspection team, the secondary machining section, and even the production line personnel. VTG, it seemed, wanted me to understand the entire value chain.

A Crash Course in Quality

Finally, after reporting back with a detailed account of my investigation, VTG's question floored me: "How sure are we that this won't happen again?" It was an early introduction to the concepts of corrective and preventive actions, terms alien to me then but ones I'd learn about in the coming weeks.

Mr. V T Govindarajan

Looking back, this was the most immersive orientation a GET could have asked for. It was a crash course in value chain mapping, understanding Critical To Quality (CTQ) parameters, and the intricate dance of commercial transactions between companies.

VTG's Leadership Legacy

VTG's leadership style, while some might call it Obsessive, ensured I dug deep, investigated across departments, and gained invaluable insights. It was a baptism by fire that served me well for years to come, shaping my understanding of the fastener industry and the importance of meticulous attention to detail – lessons that resonated as VTG went on to lead the marketing function at SFL and later became the Global Director for ELGI Equipment.

Sample

Your Story - Worksheet

Leadership Trait: Obsessive (Ensures Accuracy and High Standards)

Who: Think about someone who comes to mind when you hear the term "Obsessive" amongst your career experiences. This could be a boss, peer, colleague, subordinate, or even yourself.

Write your story: Briefly describe an anecdote (a short account of an incident) where this leader displayed obsessive behaviour related to ensuring accuracy and high standards.

What are the key learnings?

- Reflect on the positive aspects of this leader's obsessive behaviour.
- How did this leader's focus on accuracy and high standards impact you and the team?
- What did you learn about yourself and your own work ethic?

Here's an example to get you started:

Who: Mr. V.T. Govindarajan (VTG), my Marketing Manager at Sundram Fasteners Ltd.

Anecdote: As a fresh Graduate Engineer Trainee (GET), I was tasked with following up on a customer payment of Rs. 3 lakhs. VTG was meticulous in his approach. He wouldn't accept a single unanswered question, even for a small Rs. 35 discrepancy on a bill. He sent me on a company-wide chase to understand the reason behind the outstanding amount – from the finance department to the factory floor. While some might call it obsessive, it forced me to learn about the entire value chain, understand critical quality parameters, and appreciate the importance of meticulous attention to detail.

What are the key learnings?

1. **Importance of Detail:** VTG's obsessive focus on details, even a small discrepancy, revealed the interconnectedness of the entire value chain
2. **Value Chain Understanding:** "The 'wild goose chase' forced me to learn different departments' roles, leading to a deeper understanding of the entire value chain
3. **Meticulous Work Ethic:** "While initially overwhelming, VTG's approach instilled a meticulous work ethic in me, emphasizing the importance of accuracy and thoroughness in every task."

Your Story – Worksheet - 1

Leadership Trait: Obsessive (Ensures Accuracy and High Standards)

Who:
Write your story:
What are the key learnings?

Chapter 2

The Price of a Mistake

Tactful: Delivers feedback and navigates difficult situations with diplomacy

The 1990s in the Hosur factory were a world away from today's sleek offices and digital workflows. Discipline was paramount. Everyone, from the President down to the machine operators, donned identical uniforms and punched cards for attendance – no grace period for latecomers meant a half-day salary deduction.

Our days began with a regimented 5-minute warm-up exercises, followed by a flurry of activity. We cleaned our workspaces, meticulously organized the day's tasks, and then came the symphony of humming presses in the cold forging and powder metallurgy shops. As a young graduate engineer in the Production Engineering Department (PED), I was awash in a world of manual drafting, intricate tool design calculations, and hands-on learning. Experienced mentors included S L Gopi, Sampath, Jagadish Holla, Arjun & Pachaimuthu (Tool Room), fellow learners Karthikeyan, Raghu, Balaji Swaminathan (my GET mate in cold extrusion PED).

The environment was resource-constrained. We shared a mere three large drafting boards and two monochrome monitors, relics of a bygone era. Resource booking for these tools was essential, a constant dance of scheduling and coordination.

The Rookie's Blunder:

Thriving in this bustling environment, I felt like a vital cog in the machine. However, my youthful exuberance sometimes outpaced my experience. One day, tasked with designing an asymmetric cam profile tool, I made a crucial error. In the rush, I overlooked a crucial mirroring detail for the tool room component. This seemingly minor oversight had a significant impact. The fabricated tool was unusable, costing the company a substantial sum – ₹16,000, a hefty expense in those days.

Summoned to the Corner Office:

The next morning, a tremor of dread ran through me as I was called to TNS's **(T N Sathyamoorthy)** cabin, the head of PED. His reputation as a strict leader with a sharp technical mind preceded him. I braced myself for a fiery reprimand.

Tactful Intervention:

However, TNS surprised me. Instead of anger, a knowing smile played on his lips. He didn't dwell on the mistake or launch into a tirade. Instead, with a gentle manner, he asked, "What's the cost of the tool?" His voice held no accusation, just a quiet inquiry. I stammered the answer, feeling the weight of my error.

Then, a chuckle broke the tension. He asked, "How many months of your salary would it take to cover that?" (actually eight!). The question, though delivered with a light touch, effectively highlighted the gravity of the situation.

Coaching, Not Punishment:

TNS's approach wasn't simply about highlighting the mistake. He spent a considerable amount of time coaching me. He patiently explained the design process, emphasizing the importance of checks and balances before releasing drawings. He meticulously outlined how each department – design, tool room, production – was intricately linked, and how a single error could ripple through the entire production chain.

He even stressed the significance of the signature on the drawing – a symbol of ownership and responsibility that transcended mere formality. This session wasn't just about correcting a mistake; it was about building confidence.

From Fear to Growth:

The experience was a watershed moment. Over the next six months, I blossomed. The initial fear of TNS evaporated, replaced by a newfound respect. His tactful intervention fostered a sense of ownership in my work and a hunger to learn from my mistakes. We interacted frequently, engaging in discussions about metallurgical trials, machining processes, and complex tool design reviews.

Mr. T N Sathyamoorthy

The Legacy of Tact:

TNS's leadership was a masterclass intact. He navigated a potentially volatile situation with humour and transformed a potential reprimand into a valuable learning experience. His approach fostered not just accountability but also confidence, which ultimately benefitted my growth and the company's success. TNS went on to head both Cold forging & Powder metallurgy Engineering positions and then roles in Kalyani Forge and Indo MIM organizations.

This experience, a microcosm of the disciplined yet nurturing environment of the 1990s factory setting, continues to shape my approach to leadership. It serves as a constant reminder of the power of tactful communication in fostering a culture of ownership, learning, and ultimately, success.

Your Story – Worksheet - 2

Leadership Trait: Tactful (Delivers feedback and navigates difficult situations with diplomacy)

Who:
Write your story:
What are the key learnings?

Chapter 3

A Belief that Powered the Company

Unwavering: Holds firm to their values and convictions

In 1993, I found myself at a fledgling company called CG Igarashi Electric Works in Chennai. We were a ragtag team of five, tasked with setting up an entire factory for permanent magnet DC micromotors – a new technology at the time. Among us was **Uppili Santhanam**, a design head with a disarming laugh and a mind brimming with motor expertise. Unlike me, a fresh face with just four years under my belt, Uppili came seasoned from Lucas TVS.

The company was in its start-up phase, crammed into a small conference room for the first six months. We were collaborating with a Japanese company whose factories hummed in China's Shenzhen area. Back then, it was a different world – basic computers trickled in, rudimentary Excel sheets were our companions, and the trusty FX100 scientific calculator was a constant on our desks.

China Calling: A Cultural and Technical Odyssey

One early challenge came knocking – a six-month stint at the Chinese factory for me and Uppili. Now, Uppili, a devout follower of Lord Vishnu, was a strict vegetarian. The stories of Chinese cuisine filled us with apprehension. Yet, we packed our bags and embraced the unknown.

China in 1992 was a sight to behold. Infrastructure boomed, malls sprouted, and a short trip revealed the glittering modernity of Hong Kong. It was a stark contrast to what we perceived as India's state. But amidst the cultural clash, Uppili thrived. He wasn't afraid to challenge the assumptions of the Japanese team on design elements, his confidence in Indian expertise shining through. Technical discussions flowed alongside hands-on training at the factory floor, demanding hard work and creative solutions – often achieved through sign language due to the language barrier.

Back to Reality: When Blueprints Don't Translate

Back in India, we faced a new hurdle. The imported equipment and parts from China came with discrepancies between drawings, actual parts, and operational instructions. Here, Uppili's unwavering belief in his abilities truly came into play. He spearheaded crucial decision-making, preventing delays caused by back-and-forth communication with China. His approach to quality control was pragmatic – prioritizing functionality over unnecessary compliance measures, a testament to his clear vision. Heated arguments ensued, but his logic, backed by unwavering conviction, always prevailed.

The "We Know Better" Moment: Embracing the Unknown

Then came the turning point. A new, potentially huge, customer emerged, requiring motors far beyond the capabilities of our Chinese collaborators. A wave of apprehension washed over us. China was the established player, and venturing into uncharted territory seemed daunting. But Uppili, unfazed, declared, "We know better than the Chinese."

Remember, this was 1994, a time when the market was flooded with Chinese goods. Uppili's statement, fuelled by his unwavering belief in Indian potential, stood out. It wasn't arrogance, but a deep-seated conviction in our ability to excel. The company flourished, achieving success in technology, growth, market access, and global reach. While I eventually moved on, Uppili stayed put, his unwavering leadership propelling the company to even greater heights. He moved on many years later to become President of JKM Automotive. Today, he runs his own company, UB Associates, still dedicated to motor technology, now focusing on the cutting-edge e-motors for electric cars.

A Legacy of Unwavering Belief

Mr. Uppili Santhanam

Uppili's story is a testament to the power of unwavering leadership. It's not just about stubbornness; it's about holding firm to your values and convictions, particularly when faced with doubt. His unwavering belief in Indian expertise, even amidst the perceived dominance of China, became the cornerstone of our success.

Your Story – Worksheet - 3

Leadership Trait: Unwavering (Holds firm to their values and convictions)

Who:
Write your story:
What are the key learnings?

Chapter 4

A Diwali Night of Clarity

Honest: Builds trust with open communication and integrity

The year was 1995, and a wave of change was about to sweep through the Indian refrigeration industry. Whirlpool, a global leader, had just acquired Kelvinator, a beloved Indian brand. The excitement was palpable – new technology, innovative processes, and a revitalized Kelvinator were on the horizon. But beneath the surface, the reality was a factory in need of a major overhaul. Outdated equipment churned out refrigerators with slow-speed compressors and rudimentary insulation. The supply base was bloated, and inefficient workflows hampered productivity.

Enter **S S Raman** (SSR), a man with a steely gaze and a proven track record in ethical procurement. He wasn't just here to manage the procurement function; he was here to instil a culture of integrity that would transform Kelvinator. **Honesty wasn't a suggestion; it was his guiding principle.** He established clear expectations with suppliers, implementing a **zero-tolerance policy** for unethical practices. This unwavering commitment to transparency would become the bedrock of Kelvinator's revival. Mr V A Raghu (VAR) connected to TVS Family was at the helm of affairs for Whirlpool of India that time guiding all of us.

SSR, a leader who had successfully streamlined procurement processes at TVS's washing machine factories in Pondicherry, was well-equipped for the challenge. He immediately rolled up his sleeves and spearheaded a series of transformative initiatives. The outdated production lines were revamped, embracing cutting-edge Polyurethane Foam (PUF) insulation and next-generation, energy-efficient compressors. The paint shop and assembly lines received significant investments, modernizing the entire manufacturing process.

But the transformation extended beyond the factory walls. The supply base, once a tangled web of inefficiency, was undergoing a radical overhaul under SSR's leadership. He implemented a program called **Rapid Supply Base Rationalisation (RSBR)**, a strategic initiative designed to streamline the supplier network and identify the most efficient partners. This bold move, initially met with scepticism, ultimately proved to be a masterstroke. Suppliers who embraced ethical practices and aligned with Whirlpool's vision thrived, while those clinging to outdated methods were phased out.

A Test of Integrity Under Festive Lights

The festive spirit filled the air as my family and I celebrated Diwali with sweets and laughter. SSR, his wife, and their young son, Seshadri, a curious boy who would later join my team at JCB as a graduate engineer (a story for another chapter) & elder daughter had arrived to exchange Diwali greetings. We were catching up when the doorbell rang, momentarily breaking the joyous mood.

Opening the door, I found myself face-to-face with a supplier, awkwardly holding a wrapped box. "Saabji, Diwali Mubarak ho! Sirf aapke liye, thoda sa hediye" (Sir, Happy Diwali! A small gift, just for you)," he offered with a hesitant smile.

"No, thank you," I responded in English, politely declining the gift. However, the supplier, oblivious to the company's policy or the nuance of my refusal, peered past me into the house. His expression changed instantly when he spotted SSR seated in the living room. Flustered, he scurried back outside, reappearing moments later with an even bigger box! "Bade Saab ke liye bhi" (For the big sir as well)," he stammered, extending the second gift towards SSR.

SSR's reaction was swift and decisive. In his characteristic clear Hindi, he delivered a powerful message, leaving no room for misinterpretation. The supplier, clearly flustered and apologetic, retreated with both unwanted gifts.

Building Trust Through Honesty

It wasn't just about the gift; it was a powerful demonstration of our unwavering commitment to honesty. This incident resonated throughout the supply chain, fostering a more transparent and productive relationship with our suppliers.

Leading by Example

Mr. S S Raman

SSR's leadership style, though demanding at times, was a masterclass in building trust. His direct approach, combined with his unwavering honesty, created a clear standard for ethical behaviour. He led by example, proving that integrity is the cornerstone of success. The transformation of Kelvinator wouldn't have been possible without his unwavering commitment to ethical practices.

SSR went on to become the Manufacturing, Procurement & Technology (MT&P), Head for Whirlpool, where he spearheaded significant growth in the Indian market. He later moved on to head TVS Electronics, further solidifying his reputation as a visionary leader. Eight years later, our paths crossed again as I joined him at TVS Electronics. Today, SSR continues to leverage his experience, acting as a strategic consultant for many organizations and a mentor and coach for leaders across various industries.

Your Story – Worksheet - 4

Leadership Trait: Honest (Builds trust with open communication and integrity)

Who:
Write your story:
What are the key learnings?

Chapter 5

Building Strong Relationships

Networker: Builds strong relationships and fosters collaboration

My journey into the world of quality systems began in 1995 while spearheading Whirlpool Excellence System (WES) audits. Recognizing the need for a broader skillset, I embarked on a rigorous learning path acquiring certifications as a Lead Audit for Quality Management System (QMS) ISO 9000 &Environmental Management Systems (EMS) ISO 14000, Certified Quality Engineer (CQE), Certified Quality Manager (CQM), and Certified Six Sigma Black Belt (all from the American Society for Quality - ASQ) by 1998.

These qualifications, coupled with my experience in WES audits, opened doors to external audits. In 1998, I had the opportunity to conduct real-world audits on behalf of Underwriters Laboratories (UL), a globally recognized Product & Management Systems Certification Body. This experience not only involved traveling to Whirlpool factories in the US but also led me to Detroit, the auto capital of the world, for crucial certifications to QS 9000 & IATF – International Automotive Task Force Standard IATF 16949

Earning the QS9000 Auditor Certification:

Obtaining the QS9000 auditor certification was a significant milestone. Mastering complex topics like MSA (Measurement System Analysis), FMEA (Failure Mode and Effects Analysis), SPC (Statistical Process Control), APQP (Advanced Product Quality Planning), and PPAP (Production Part Approval Process) through exams was a demanding yet rewarding experience. J Chandrasekar (JC) from UL was a key mentor to me those days.

Building a Network for Success:

This period also marked the beginning of a remarkable partnership with **B B Gupta**, fondly known as BBG.

Mr. B B Gupta

BBG embodied the essence of a true networker. His magnetic personality, coupled with his friendly and approachable demeanor, allowed him to strike up conversations with anyone, anywhere on Technical; Financials & Families what endeared to the listeners. He possessed an uncanny ability to connect with people from all walks of life, from Top management to Frontline Employees.

Patriotism and Networking:

BBG's unwavering patriotism was evident in his enthusiasm for flying the Indian Flag during audits all over the World – Australia; Singapore; Samoa; Pakistan; Malaysia & most importantly South Africa. He passionately advocated for Indian potential to become a global manufacturing hub. His networking prowess extended beyond mere connections; he meticulously followed up, ensuring strong and lasting relationships especially in South Africa where he has become the most preferred partner to all Automotive & Non-Automotive Organizations from Europe; Japan; Korea; China & USA. Along with his Spouse Dr. Tripta Gupta he was invited in South Africa to unfurl National Flag of India on 15th August. Their Organization ASR South Africa is the most preferred Certification Body in this country with almost zero attrition in last 25 years of being there.

Memorable Audits and BBG's Expertise:

Several unique audits conducted alongside BBG stand out in my memory. One such instance involved Amar Singh Chawal Wala Foods in Amritsar & Amira Foods in Pataudi Road - companies exporting Basmati rice. This audit revealed the intricate processes involved in Rice Procurement to Production; Testing from raw materials to post-cooking characteristics like elongation and aroma. BBG's unparalleled network within the rice industry allowed him to leverage my technical expertise during the audits, highlighting the company's strengths and potential areas for improvement.

A Networker's Legacy:

Another unforgettable audit took place at Arvind Eye Hospitals in Madurai. Their cataract surgery procedures resembled a well-oiled assembly line, showcasing their advanced practices. Unfortunately, BBG suffered a fall from a hotel balcony during this trip, resulting in a major fracture. Even from his hospital bed, his networking spirit remained unfazed as he continued to connect with businesses. He got up after 7 months in bed and did the audits walking on 2 Crutches for almost all the months in the

Year 2001. BBG is having a full-length Steel rod in his leg from foot to knee even now since May 2000.

BBG's leadership style exemplifiesthe power of a Networker; Performance with honesty of purpose & under commitment – building strong relationships and fostering collaboration for mutual benefit.

BBG continues to lead his networking skills spreading name & fame of India. Both BBG & Dr Gupta still travels across the world auditing & certifying organizations & promoting Indian excellence completing 75 years in their life journey this year in 2024.

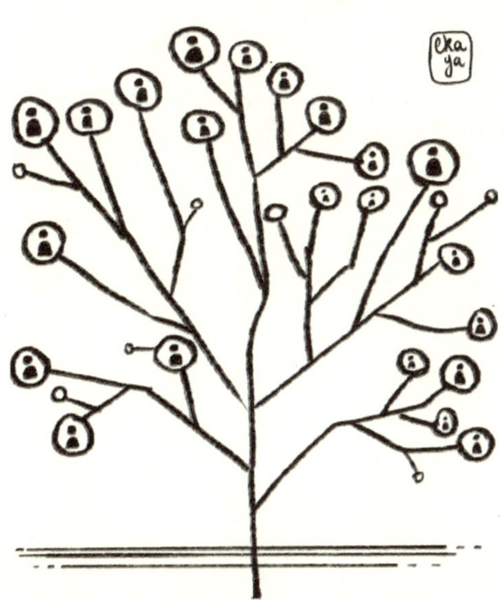

Your Story – Worksheet - 5

Leadership Trait: Networker: Builds strong relationships and fosters collaboration

Who:
Write your story:
What are the key learnings?

Chapter 6

Facing the Storm

Fearless: Makes tough decisions and isn't afraid of challenges

The acquisition was a whirlwind. Whirlpool, divesting its compressor division, handed the reins to Tecumseh. We, the new team, inherited a storm brewing beneath the surface - a large workforce, financial losses, and whispers of a militant union. Leading this team, with a steady hand and a wealth of experience, was Vipin Sondhi, or VS as we called him. A leader I will delve deeper into in a later chapter, VS's strategic vision and unwavering support would prove invaluable in the coming months.

Enter **Harendra Kumar**, or HK as we called him. Head of Procurement, but a man of multi-tasks, he wasn't one for mincing words. His reputation preceded him - strong relationships within the city, a calm hand in negotiations, and an unwavering commitment to clear communication. HK's fearlessness manifested in his ability to make tough decisions and ensure everyone understood the reasoning behind them. Of course Saumen Chakraborty (SC), the then Group HR head was completely extending the necessary support and leading the strategies.

Then, disaster struck. An accident in the factory ignited a powder keg of emotions. The union, as we'd feared, called for a strike. The city, already abuzz with rumours, erupted in protest. In the face of this storm, HK, with a heavy heart, made the difficult call to lock down the factory.

Setback though it was, the team didn't wallow. We scrambled. HK, ever the leader, spearheaded the outside operations. Inside the locked factory, a skeletal crew, led by Vikram Prabhu, held the fort, maintaining critical machinery. Vikram, another key player in this story, will be covered in a separate chapter. The situation demanded a multi-pronged approach, and HK, a master of juggling, rose to the occasion.

- We had a new product, the MLA, breathing down our necks. With limited access to the factory, launching it on time meant relying heavily on engineering drawings and analysis.
- Simultaneously, we began the herculean task of transferring essential machinery from an old Whirlpool factory to bolster our capabilities at Tecumseh Ballabgarh.
- Looming large was the sensitive issue of manpower reduction. A golden handshake program was rolled out, a necessary but painful step towards financial viability.

HK, ever the fearless negotiator, along with SC, used his strong relationships and direct communication style to bridge the gap with the union. The discussions were tense, emotions raw, but after six long months, a resolution was reached. The factory gates swung open once more. Reopening wasn't a magic bullet. The human cost of the crisis was evident in the distraught faces of those who lost their jobs. But HK, with unwavering determination, kept the team unified under the guidance of VS & SC. Slowly, steadily, normalcy returned. Within six months, the factory hummed with activity once more, a testament to the resilience of the team and the unwavering leadership of HK.

Building on Success: A Legacy of Leadership

Mr. Harendra Kumar

VS, SC, HK, and all the other senior leaders who weathered this storm went on to steer the company to success. HK had a successful stint at Tectumseh before moving on to transform the Supply Chain Management (SCM) function at Bharti Airtel. Subsequently a long stint at Tower Vision India as Senior Vice President. This experience underscored the importance of fearless leadership and the ripple effect it can have on an organization and the careers of those involved.

Your Story – Worksheet - 6

Leadership Trait: Fearless (Makes tough decisions and isn't afraid of challenges)

Who:
Write your story:
What are the key learnings?

Chapter 7

The Temple of Work

Grateful: Appreciates contributions and fosters a positive environment

Setting the Stage: A Leader Who Walks the Talk

K.S. Madhavan, affectionately known as KSM, wasn't your typical Managing Director. He wasn't one for corner offices or hierarchical distance. For KSM, the factory floor at Tecumseh in Hyderabad was a temple of work, and he was its devoted leader. A firm believer in world-class shop floor culture, he championed the implementation of Japanese tools and techniques to foster a truly exceptional workplace.

The Pillars of Productivity: 5S and Kaizen

KSM's philosophy was simple: a clean, organized workspace breeds efficiency and quality. He emphasized the 5S principles (Sort, Systematic Arrangement, Shine, Standardize, Sustain) as the cornerstone of work ethic. Japanese economy could be changed from unbearable losses after the Second World War to the Second Best Economy in the world in a short period using the principles & disciplines of 5S as foundation – not just in factories but across the entire society – on streets, social establishments, Government offices etc., A clean and organized space, with standardized methods and readily available tools, naturally led to improved productivity, quality consistency, safety, employee morale, and overall satisfaction.

He believed that Kaizen, the concept of continuous improvement, was the lifeblood of a factory striving for customer satisfaction in terms of quality, cost, and delivery (QCD).

Leading by Example: A Culture of Recognition

KSM wasn't just a preacher; he was a diligent practitioner. His desk was always impeccably organized, reflecting his belief in streamlined processes. He championed a robust Reward & Recognition program, emphasizing timely recognition and consistent monitoring. His core belief: a positive workplace leads to happy employees, and happy employees produce better products.

Beyond the Shop Floor: A Focus on Wellbeing

KSM's leadership extended beyond the shop floor. He understood the importance of a healthy and positive work environment. The company canteen was a point of pride. The ambience, cleanliness, and quality of food were constantly monitored. This focus on employee wellbeing resonated in the new canteen built at the Ballabgarh factory, featuring comfortable seating, modern equipment, and a focus on minimizing food waste.

An organisation's transformation can be achieved with total support from each employee using the principles of TEI (Total Employee Involvement), not just with the efforts of Top Leadership team. It was made possible by KSM by sharing a small part of the

'Value Added' with the workers and staff who contributed directly to it.

A Radical, Yet Rewarding, Approach: Linking Salary to Performance

KSM wasn't afraid to shake things up. He introduced a radical salary policy – a monthly variable component of Rs. 500 tied directly to workplace performance. This included factors like punctuality, adherence to 5S principles, productivity, participation in suggestion schemes, and safety practices. This innovative approach, met with initial apprehension, garnered surprising support from the union and employees alike. The lure of a larger pay check at the end of the month spurred a positive change in behaviour across all levels. The focus shifted to workplace improvement, and the company's business performance saw a dramatic rise.

This revolutionary policy, a brainchild of KSM, cemented his belief in the power of sustained reward and recognition as the cornerstone of any thriving work culture.

Grateful Leadership: The Legacy of KSM

Mr. K S Madhavan

KSM's leadership embodied the essence of gratitude. He appreciated contributions, fostered a positive environment, and motivated his employees to excel. Leading by example, he created a culture of continuous improvement that propelled the company towards excellence. As someone who had the privilege of working under him,

I witnessed first-hand the profound impact he had on my own career path. Leaders like KSM leave an indelible mark, not just on companies, but on the lives of those they inspire. His dedication to creating a world-class work environment laid the foundation for further success, leading him to establish the successful Kaizen Institute, which continues to deliver impressive results through its meticulously trained consultants. KSM's legacy exemplifies the power of grateful leadership in building a thriving and successful organization.

Your Story – Worksheet - 7

Leadership Trait: Grateful (Appreciates contributions and fosters a positive environment)

Who:
Write your story:
What are the key learnings?

Chapter 8

The Power of Fairness and Respect

Just : Makes fair decisions and treats everyone with respect

The Quiet Strength of VRR

There are leaders who elevate management practices to an art form. One such leader, fondly remembered as our "Quality Guru," was **V Raghavendra Rao** (VRR). Soft-spoken yet firm, VRR possessed a quiet strength that commanded respect. While his usual demeanour was calm, his occasional bursts of controlled intensity served as powerful wake-up calls, instantly highlighting the folly of our "un-quality" actions.

VRR, stationed in Hyderabad, oversaw the group's overall quality, acting as my functional boss while I reported administratively to VS. His initial visits were monthly, transitioning to quarterly as his confidence in our systems grew. These visits were eagerly awaited, as they presented a condensed learning opportunity within a short timeframe. It was fascinating to see such an exceptional leader emerge from a traditional organization like Shriram Refrigeration. Unlike their western counterparts who heavily promoted every initiative, Shriram Refrigeration nurtured a culture where successful shop-floor practices thrived quietly, unnamed and uncelebrated.

VRR's Uncanny Observations

VRR possessed an uncanny observational power. Nothing escaped his keen senses. He could detect compressor shell welding defects by smell, and assess paint quality by touch or simply running his nails across the surface. He shared a memorable anecdote about a quality head known for his daily ritual of using a 3M tape test on painted parts. This head invariably found paint traces on the tape, leading to part rejection. One day, to VRR's surprise, the tape was clean. With a stern voice, he ordered, "Reject the tape!"

Our meticulous record-keeping practices, a habit instilled by VRR, ensured that observations during audits translated into control systems for sustained improvement. These practices, like wedges on a steep slope, prevented regression.

The Importance of Fairness and Respect

VRR embodied fairness. He was approachable anytime, anywhere, offering a listening ear and a solution for every grievance. Respect for every individual was his core value. Even when addressing serious issues, he ensured the focus remained on the process or system, treating the situation as a human problem rather than assigning blame. His philosophy emphasized the importance of well-defined processes and systems as shields to protect products from defects.

In early 2001, during the launch of new models, we faced high PPM rejection rates. A customer-returned compressor was dissected in our "cut-open shop," a place resembling a mortuary where we, the quality doctors, performed post-mortems. VRR, our chief doctor, meticulously trained us on proper dissection procedures to ensure no crucial clues were missed. Daily visits to the cut-open shop were mandatory for all, serving as a stark reflection of our process control and product maturity. VRR's vision was to achieve "zero compressor" rejection, signifying zero PPM from customer fallout data. I can't forget the crucial role played by D S P Rao and his talented quality team, including C S Bhatt, Vinod Aggarwal, Rajpal, Damodaran, Anu Dhar, Rajesh Rajput, Anil Dwivedi, Joydip Dutta, Madhukar Sinha, and Vishwanath. All of them were mentored by VRR and DSP to become expert quality professionals.

After two years of relentless effort, we achieved this goal, a celebration shared by everyone. VRR's success lay in his ability to involve every individual in the factory, carrying them all along on this journey. This leadership style demands a high degree of trust and the unshakeable belief that the leader will always be fair and impartial.

VRR's Leadership Legacy

Mr. V Raghavendra Rao

VRR's leadership was characterized by a relentless pursuit of quality and a disciplined approach to management. He believed that quality should permeate every aspect of the company, from products and services to people, processes, systems, and the environment. VRR instituted innovative practices like Zero PPM days to ensure customer satisfaction and emphasized quality and safety in production meetings, a departure from industry norms. His unique perspective as a leader in operations, HR, and quality allowed him to seamlessly integrate these functions and ensure that quality was at the heart of every decision. VRR recognized the interconnectedness of quality, cost, delivery, safety, environment, and employee morale, and emphasized the importance of maintaining a healthy balance in all these areas. Under his leadership, Tecumseh India achieved international recognition for its environmental compliance and incorporated quality standards into employee wage agreements. VRR's commitment to holistic employee development was evident in his implementation of functional job rotation programs.

A decade later, leading a large team tackling field quality problems at JCB, I realized the invaluable driving skills VRR had instilled in me. He had equipped me to be an "unconscious driver," confidently steering the company towards the right destination. VRR's leadership perfectly exemplified the trait of being "Just" – making fair decisions and treating everyone with respect.

Your Story – Worksheet - 8

Leadership Trait: Just (Makes fair decisions and treats everyone with respect)

Who:
Write your story:
What are the key learnings?

Chapter 9

Taking Ownership

Responsible: Takes ownership of actions and decisions

Working as a woman in a leadership position within the Indian manufacturing industry during those times presented unique challenges. Balancing work demands with family life often meant women shouldered the heavy burden of responsibilities at both home and the factory. My subordinate, **Chitra Verma** (CV), Head of Design Department, exemplified this kind of leader who embraced responsibility with unwavering commitment.

A Natural Leader with Deep Expertise

CV possessed a natural aptitude for ownership. Clear-headed and decisive, she readily took full responsibility for any assigned task. Her extensive experience in refrigerator design and development at Whirlpool before joining Tecumseh for compressor design was invaluable.

I recall a conversation with Dr. George Gatecliff, Tecumseh's Global Engineering Head, who emphasized, "The design of a compressor crankshaft is not simply a matter of life and death; it's far more than that." Unlike other electrical appliances, a hermetically sealed compressor in a refrigerator operates continuously, with a 24/7 duty cycle except for brief temperature-controlled cycles.

Additionally, it's a completely sealed system filled with lubricant oil for its lifespan, unlike a car engine where oil changes are part of routine maintenance. In a compressor, the refrigerant gas and oil remain sealed throughout its life, only being opened during rare cases of field service for low or no cooling issues. Therefore, designing a reliable refrigerator compressor is absolutely crucial. Given the critical nature of her role, CV understood the immense responsibility she held.

Leading Design Through Regulatory Change

The industry was undergoing sweeping changes in regulatory compliance due to growing environmental concerns and efforts to protect the ozone layer. Initiatives like the Montreal and Kyoto protocols significantly impacted the design team, necessitating major changes in cooling cycles, pressures, temperatures, and a crucial shift from mineral to synthetic oil for CFC-free systems.

These changes demanded a staggering number of design iterations and validation tests. Our life test labs operated around the clock, and CV actively collaborated with our Ann Arbor engineers to design more testing equipment. This included motor lock testers, low voltage start testers, newer calorimeters, accelerated life test rigs, and customized test cycle conditions to expedite approvals. Every design change release note bearing CV's signature carried immense weight, a responsibility she shouldered with unwavering confidence.

Adapting to New Challenges: The BEE Regulations

Just as we believed the climate change-related challenges were behind us, we were struck by the introduction of BEE (Bureau of Energy Efficiency) regulations in 2003. This new system mandated star ratings for home appliances based on their energy efficiency. For compressors, power consumption and cooling system efficiency were measured by the EER (Energy Efficiency Ratio). India's unique challenge lies in its voltage fluctuations, ranging from 140 to 240 volts, unlike the narrow voltage bands in western countries. While voltage stabilizers are recommended for purchase, their enforcement is lax, essentially forcing compressors to operate across this wide voltage range, hindering the achievement of higher EERs.

Rising to the EER Challenge: The THK Project

Our evaluation of the current MLA platform revealed that refrigerators using our compressors would achieve a maximum of 1-star rating under the new system. This necessitated the introduction of a new compressor platform – the THK technology, housed in Tecumseh's Brazil factory.

I transitioned to head the THK project, with CV continuing to manage the design release of the existing platform while taking on the additional responsibility of the THK platform as well. Vikram Prabhu joined the project to lead production release accountability. Over a three-year period, I undertook 13 trips to Brazil, conducting numerous tests and trials to ensure the THK platform met Indian operating conditions and achieved higher EER levels. Two years of rigorous development yielded successful THK prototypes, placing a double burden on CV's shoulders as she now had to manage production design releases for both platforms.

A Leader Worthy of Admiration

Ms. Chitra Verma

CV epitomized the spirit of a true workaholic and a dedicated leader. She possessed a deep understanding of the gravity of situations, readily shouldered responsibility, and consistently delivered successful results. I am grateful to have had such a leader on my team, and fortunate to have witnessed others like her across various departments, be it quality or engineering.

Her story exemplifies the rare breed of leaders who embrace responsibility and navigate challenges with unwavering commitment. While my experience collaborating with VP on the THK platform's production rollout merits its own chapter, this chapter serves to highlight the invaluable contribution of leaders like CV, a true gem within the industry.

Your Story – Worksheet - 9

Leadership Trait: Responsible (Takes ownership of actions and decisions)

Who:
Write your story:
What are the key learnings?

Chapter 10

The Whisper in the House

Knowledgeable: Possesses expertise and fosters a culture of learning

Ten chapters into this exploration of leadership traits, a seemingly ordinary appliance – a refrigerator – takes centre stage. This story exemplifies the power of a knowledgeable leader who fosters a culture of learning within their team. It's a testament to **Anupam Gupta** (AG), a leader who left a lasting impression with his unique ability to combine deep knowledge with a passion for shared learning.

The Unexpected Complaint: Noise and Its Impact

It all began with a rather unexpected complaint from a customer in Mumbai. Their son's studies were being disrupted by the persistent hum of the refrigerator compressor. This anecdote, while seemingly insignificant, highlighted the often-unforeseen consequences of product design choices, particularly when it comes to noise levels in household appliances.

Understanding the science of sound measurement became crucial. We delved into the world of decibel ranges, anechoic chambers, and the need to control specific frequencies for optimal performance. This quest for silence led to the development of a three-part plastic suction muffler for the compressor.

Enter AG: The Walking Encyclopaedia and His KKD Philosophy

Then came AG, our new VP of Operations, who quickly earned the nickname "walking encyclopaedia" for his vast knowledge base. His leadership style, however, went beyond just possessing knowledge. AG championed his "KKD" (Kar Ke Dekho – Do & See for Yourself) philosophy, which emphasized the importance of practical application. He wouldn't just offer solutions; he encouraged us to experiment, learn, and find solutions ourselves.

The Challenge of the Muffler: Glue and the Search for Scalability

Our team encountered a hurdle in the assembly process of the three-part muffler. While a special glue identified with Henkel seemed promising for lab testing, concerns arose about its scalability for mass production. We needed a solution that could handle the demands of high-volume manufacturing.

AG's Intervention: The Power of a Well-Placed Suggestion

During a casual visit to our lab, AG, in his usual style, threw out a seemingly random suggestion – ultrasonic welding. This unfamiliar concept caught us off guard. We were accustomed to techniques like seam welding and furnace brazing for steel and copper tubes, but ultrasonic welding for plastics? It was a whole new territory.

Embracing the Challenge: Learning from the Automotive Industry

Embracing AG's KKD challenge, we embarked on a learning journey. We studied how ultrasonic welding was applied in the automotive industry, its potential for our project, and the technicalities involved. We designed joints specifically for ultrasonic welding and identified suppliers who could conduct trials.

The initial prototypes were a setback. Leaks and inconsistencies in the sealing process highlighted the complexity of the new technology. Discouraged, we approached AG with our half-hearted results.

Halfway There: The Introduction of Lantern Rings

Instead of disappointment, AG surprised us with a hearty laugh. "You've crossed half the bridge," he declared. "Now, let's learn about lantern rings." This previously unknown term sent us on a new research quest. We consulted with plastic precision moulders, finally understanding the concept of interlocking grooves that, combined with ultrasonic welding, would create a perfect seal.

The Power of Shared Learning: AG's Legacy

Mr. Anupam Gupta

This experience with AG was a turning point. He wasn't just a leader who possessed knowledge; he was a catalyst for continuous learning within the team. He demonstrated that knowledge is not a finite resource – sharing it only enriches everyone involved.

AG's commitment to learning extended far beyond the factory walls. AG moved to a new assignment with an Automotive Component group, where he led a team of young engineers to develop the now familiar JBM Bus, a world-class modern City vehicle.

After successfully battling Cancer in 2012, he changed tracks to pursue his passion of Wildlife Photography. Now devotes his energies to accompanying & guiding youngsters into Wildlife and Astro-photography. He also counsels Cancer Patients on how to manage treatment, and Mentor Start-ups in diverse fields of Tensegrity Structures & Space-Frames, EV Chargers, and Hybrid Cooling Systems.

AG's story serves as a testament to the power of a knowledgeable leader who fosters a culture of learning. It's a reminder that true leadership is not just about giving orders or possessing knowledge, but about empowering others to learn, experiment, and grow.

Your Story – Worksheet - 10

Leadership Trait: Knowledgeable (Possesses expertise and fosters a culture of learning)

Who:
Write your story:
What are the key learnings?

Chapter 11

Building on Passion

Energized: Infuses the team with enthusiasm and motivation

This project was a rollercoaster. Here I was, leading the Design Engineering team, partnered with **Vikram Prabhu**, or VP as everyone called him. He came from electronics engineering, a meticulous guy with an eagle eye for detail in machine drawings. We were an unlikely pair, but together we shouldered the responsibility of the entire THK project – a new platform crucial for the company, meeting future regulations and market demands. It was a big deal, a significant investment, and we were a small team, just five of us, leading the charge.

A Collaborative Effort

Think supporting cast – production, quality, design, purchasing, finance, HR – the whole crew from the current platform. We had to collaborate seamlessly, couldn't afford to come across as arrogant young leaders pushing this "future" vision. We were young, me at 36 and VP at a fresh 32, compared to the seasoned heads of other departments. But we had built a strong connection with the Brazil facility, where part of the technology transfer and innovation would happen.

The Power of Clear Direction

VP, bless his systematic soul, believed in clear direction. We started with a 100-page document, a bible outlining everything – assumptions, targets, our entire approach. It became our reference point, a beacon in the storm of product development. Let me tell you, there were storms. Technical hurdles had a way of dragging you down, making you feel isolated. But VP, that guy... his optimism was infectious. Our friendship, forged during those long flights to Brazil and exploring Sao Paulo together, became our anchor. We weren't just colleagues, we had each other's backs.

VP lead a powerful team of Sanjay Garg and Suresh Nair (apart from Design side Sandeep Saxena – the silent performer), other two youngsters who powered all their engineering expertise cylinders during this project. These two hard working and committed members, always wanted the best facilities for the lowest price and constantly looked out for good technical and commercial deals. They also were fascinated by the Brazilian partner / International technology and loved the collaboration and learning. Equally vociferous in getting the best outcomes for the shopfloor, they grounded VP and me to the practical needs from the production process. Through it all, they were supportive, open to challenges and thrived in difficult situations. The project was manageable and went smoother due to their contributions.

Leading by Example: Transparency and Engagement

Then came the machinery procurement. VP, ever the detail-oriented guy, put together these thorough RFQ packages, demanding specific productivity and quality levels. It ruffled some feathers across departments, this new way of doing things. But that's where his high energy came in. He wouldn't take no for an answer. He'd engage with everyone, from top management to the guys on the ground, explain the logic, share the details – complete transparency.

Overcoming Resistance

It wasn't easy. Redefining productivity norms, documented station-wise for the current platform, meant lower output. People feared job losses, resistance was natural. But VP, with his trademark patience and persistence, brought everyone to the table. Discussions became enthusiastic, not antagonistic. Trial runs with the new equipment and jigs proved the feasibility of the new standards.

Mr. Vikram Prabhu

One outstanding feature of the TH team was the volatile technical arguments and sometime yelling. Since the product and project transfer included a lot of new features and technology, differences in expectations, opinions and experience were common among the group members. The willingness to confront these differences (rather than blindly doing what the boss wanted) was a testament to the non-hierarchical nature of the team no matter the designations. Even younger members felt a confidence and an equal right to defend their views and opinions loudly in the face of a technical challenge. This was valued and respected throughout and caused loud noises sometimes from the project office but much better long term and rational outcomes for the project. The differences never became personal and every stiff argument normally ended with smiles shortly after.

Beyond Technical Expertise: The Value of Negotiation

There were other challenges, of course. Remember the Bill of Material cost? A significant reduction was crucial. It was our responsibility, engineering and purchasing, to negotiate with vendors and bring those costs down. We were on track, but then things started to slip. VP, ever accountable as the project lead, jumped in. He motivated the purchasing team to think long-term, consider volume-based contracts. It meant sacrificing some initial cost reduction, but the roadmap for future savings was clear.

The Energized Leader: A Catalyst for Success

These are just a few examples of VP's boundless energy, his unwavering ability to motivate and keep everyone enthusiastic. He was the epitome of an Energized leader, a guy who could inspire a team to achieve the extraordinary. And his dedication went beyond the project. After seeing THK through to production success, he moved on to Carrier and finally ended up heading Ethics & Compliance for their South Asia Pacific region. That's the kind of leader VP was – a spark that ignited a fire within the team.

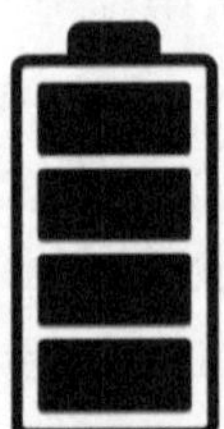

Your Story – Worksheet - 11

Leadership Trait: Energized (Infuses the team with enthusiasm and motivation)

Who:
Write your story:
What are the key learnings?

Chapter 12

From Qualifications to Capability

Qualified: Possesses the skills and experience to lead effectively

This chapter explores the importance of a Qualified leader - someone who possesses the skills and experience to lead effectively. We'll follow the story of **Lakshmi Ranganathan** (Laks), who exemplifies this trait through her work on various quality improvement initiatives.

Building the Framework: A Foundation for Success

In 2006, I transitioned from Tecumseh to TVS. Yearning for a return to my roots, I re-joined TVS Electronics under my former Whirlpool boss, SSR, who was now the Executive Director. Taking on a core TQM role based in Chennai, I found myself leading multiple Total Employee Involvement (TEI) initiatives. One of the key aspects involved deploying Six Sigma practices to drive the TVS Operating System Model (TOS) spearheaded by Dr K Prasanna Sai. It was during this period that Laks joined my team as a leader.

Laks was a powerhouse of qualifications, with an insatiable thirst for knowledge. Together, we embarked on building a training framework for Six Sigma. Her natural teaching ability shone through as she delivered complex Six Sigma lectures with ease. We structured the program into YB (Yellow Belt), GB (Green Belt), and BB (Black Belt) levels, with BB certification being the most challenging to achieve. Thankfully, I possessed the necessary expertise due to my prior ASQ-CSBB qualification.

Bridging the Gap: From Qualifications to Experience

The cornerstone of Six Sigma training is a solid foundation in statistics. Effective instruction hinges on both qualifications and the ability to apply those concepts practically. While Laks had the academic credentials and teaching skills, she lacked experience in our specific industry. However, her agility shone through as she capitalized on various opportunities to gain practical experience. We were fortunate to have a parallel Kaizen program running, which provided a platform for building case studies and deploying statistical tools for the YB program. These tools primarily involved hypothesis testing to validate improvements.

A particularly memorable project involved a successful Kaizen Blitz program with Laks, where we reorganized the entire shop floor. This resulted in a visible transformation of the layout and process flow, leading to reduced manpower, lower inventory levels, and improved quality and throughput. Lean tools provided another avenue for Laks to acquire real-world examples. By connecting different concepts, we were able to build a cohesive narrative for TQM.

Building the Culture : Quality & Lean six sigma in Organization DNA

Embedding Lean Six Sigma and a culture of quality into organization's DNA required strategic approach that aligns with company's mission, values and long-term goals involving employees across levels. We provided Lean Six Sigma training at all levels, conducted Quality Circles and Quality Month celebration. November Quality Month celebration at TVS was a great way to engage employees, reinforce importance of quality and helped to promote continuous improvement culture. The events included but not limited to – sharing daily quality tips, conducting quality tools training, rewarding for best 5S workplace, promoting projects, conducting quality tools related quiz and Kaizen blitz.

Mentorship and Shared Experiences:

Multiplying Knowledge

Our journey was further enriched by the guidance of two Japanese Gurus who visited us twice a year for in-depth discussions and shop floor visits. Professor Washio, an expert in design methodologies, reviewed all NPI (New Product Introduction) projects and existing product failure modes. Professor Tsuda, a manufacturing process quality expert, analysed customer and process quality metrics, as well as various improvement projects. Laks and the quality team played a pivotal role in coordinating these visits, and these interactions significantly enriched our collective experiences.

The Deming Prize Challenge: A Holistic Approach

We then embarked on a Deming Prize initiative, a comprehensive program fostering stakeholder engagement. Laks shouldered a significant portion of the workload, expertly balancing her time and efforts. Imagine a juggler – without the necessary skills and experience, their performance would be riddled with errors. My time at TVS Electronics may have been brief, but my experience working with Laks was both unforgettable and rewarding.

Ms. Lakshmi Ranganathan

Laks exemplifies the "Qualified" leader. Her combination of academic credentials and her ability to leverage opportunities to gain practical experience solidified her expertise. She went on to lead numerous initiatives at TVS Electronics before moving on to spearhead large-scale transformation programs at Nokia. Currently, she is a senior leader at an International Bank heading Process Transformation initiatives.

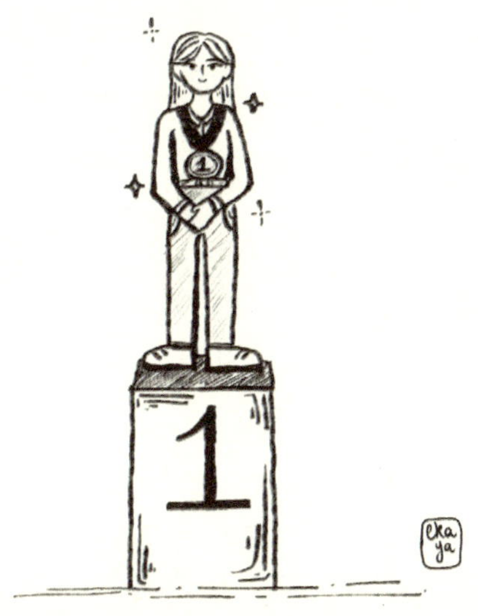

Your Story – Worksheet - 12

Leadership Trait: Qualified (Possesses the skills and experience to lead effectively)

Who:
Write your story:
What are the key learnings?

Chapter 13

The Spark Within

Inspirational: Motivates and empowers others to achieve their best

This chapter delves into the essence of an Inspirational leader – someone who motivates and empowers others to achieve their full potential. We'll explore this concept through the remarkable journey of **Vipin Sondhi** (VS), a leader who ignited a fire within his team and the entire industry.

Building a Culture of Ownership: Inspiration Through Empowerment

Returning to North India in 2007, I found myself reunited with VS, who had taken the helm at JCB India as MD & CEO. I joined him to lead Quality and Business Excellence initiatives. Though I'd mentioned him in previous chapters, I hadn't done justice to his profound impact. VS stands tall as one of India's most inspirational leaders, a man who spearheaded decades of transformative growth (1990-2020). His vision not only propelled JCB India but also laid a strong foundation for the "Make in India" initiative, fostering domestic manufacturing and establishing India as an export hub.

VS's leadership style was meticulously structured. Every Monday, without fail, he convened his Executive Leadership Team for meetings. These were forums for deep dives into company performance, where he actively encouraged participation. Functional heads and junior leaders presented their projects and progress, fostering a culture of shared ownership and involvement. Under his guidance, I spearheaded a Business Excellence initiative that culminated in a prestigious CII award a few years later. For VS, the focus was never the award itself, but building a robust foundation of excellence in every aspect of the business. He used to meticulously review the progress with the core Cross Functional Team (CFT) comprising of emerging leaders Sujan Mukherjee (HR), Sivarama Krishna (Service), Puneet Vidyarthi (Marketing), Dinesh Parashar (Design), Lokesh Pandey (Quality), Pradeep Kathuria (Finance), Navneet Sethi (Manufacturing), Gunjan Malhotra (Manufacturing Engineering), Sanjay Kathuria (Operations), Dheeraj Verma (EHS), Bagavathy Appan (Purchase), Pratap Joshi (IT), providing invaluable mentoring to their careers.

Beyond the Company Walls: Inspiring Broader Impact

VS's influence extended far beyond JCB India. A recipient of the CII Young Manager award early in his career, he went on to lead various industry committees. During my interactions with other industry leaders on these committees, I witnessed the immense respect they held for VS. His words and wisdom inspired countless individuals across diverse businesses to achieve extraordinary feats.

Here are a few examples of VS's wide-ranging external engagements:

- **Bharatiya Yuva Shakti Trust (BYST):** This initiative empowers microentrepreneurs. In 2008, I participated in a BYST Business Ideas contest that culminated in successful case studies presented to Prince Charles during his visit to Chandigarh.
- **CII Water Institute:** As Chairperson, VS championed commendable water conservation initiatives.
- **Excon India:** VS served as Chairman of India's largest construction machinery exhibition for a decade. This CII Initiative became an example of how CEOs of an industry collectively work in unison for the growth of the industry.
- **National Steering Committees:** VS actively participated in numerous national steering committees and government initiatives.

It's truly astounding how VS managed to juggle these diverse, impactful endeavours while simultaneously steering JCB India to unparalleled leadership.

Building a Legacy of Inspiration: From Employees to Communities

VS was a firm believer in investing in the future, be it dealerships, factories, infrastructure, or people. This forward-thinking approach instilled a deep sense of motivation within the organization, encouraging employees to stay on and contribute to JCB's success story. Under his leadership, JCB's factory footprint expanded significantly, culminating in the world's largest backhoe plant at Jaipur. He also transformed JCB India into a major global export hub.

VS actively fostered a spirit of community among dealerships. He personally participated in motivating and inspiring them to excel. These efforts culminated in dealer conferences held in exciting locations like Las Vegas, Cairo, Shanghai, and Cape Town. These events fostered a sense of shared purpose and instilled a global mindset within the JCB India network.

VS's commitment extended beyond the company walls. His CSR initiatives, focused on community engagement, resulted in significant development in villages and schools around the company's factories. His dedication to supplier partnerships was equally noteworthy. Yearly supplier conferences brought hundreds of partners together, fostering a sense of community despite their competitive nature.

A Celebration of Success: Inspiring the Team and Their Families

Mr. Vipin Sondhi

One of the most inspiring moments for senior leadership occurred on New Year's Day. JCB India celebrated the year's beginning with festivities at its factories, inviting employee families. These day-long events included engaging activities for spouses, children, and other family members, creating lasting memories for all. And the story doesn't end there! VS hosted a special evening dinner for senior leadership and their spouses. He would meticulously prepare presentations with videos, highlighting each leader's contributions and expressing his gratitude. He then outlined his vision for the year ahead, further solidifying their commitment to achieving shared goals.

VS's inspirational impact is truly rare, a shining example of leadership that empowers and motivates individuals to reach their full potential. His journey continued as he went on to become MD & CEO of Ashok Leyland. Even in his post-retirement phase, he remains actively involved as Independent Director, Chairmen technology councils for CII and serving as Chairperson for NBQP-QCI (Quality Council of India) and with academic institutions like IISc Bengaluru, his alma mater IIT Delhi and the Lawrence School, Sanawar.

Your Story – Worksheet - 13

Leadership Trait: Inspirational (Motivates and empowers others to achieve their best)

Who:
Write your story:
What are the key learnings?

Chapter 14

The Power of Stories

Memorable: Makes a lasting positive impact on those they lead

Great leaders leave a mark. They inspire, challenge, and shape the people they work with. **Alan Blake** (AB), then Global CEO of JCB, was one such leader. His ability to connect through storytelling left a lasting impression on me, not just personally, but also on the way we approached quality at JCB India.

From Chaos to Discipline: The Seed of Change

AB wasn't one for formalities. He'd strike up conversations, often ending with his signature, "One more thing..." These seemingly casual anecdotes were packed with meaning. During one visit, he expressed his concern about the stark difference between the order he saw in Japanese factories and the apparent chaos on the streets of Delhi. This dichotomy, he believed, was a barrier to achieving true discipline within the workplace.

AB's admiration for Japanese work culture was evident. He frequently referenced the Toyota Production System (TPS) and its emphasis on shop floor discipline. While I agreed with the philosophy, I pointed out the challenge of adapting a theoretical framework to the realities of our industry. This sparked a conversation that led to the birth of the JCB Production System – a system tailored to our specific needs. We documented existing processes, identified metrics, and created visual aids to guide workers.

Beyond the Bookshelf: From Checklists to ICU-Inspired Quality

AB's love for books became a bridge between us. We'd exchange recommendations, leading to in-depth discussions. Once, he requested a synopsis of Atul Gawande's "Checklist Manifesto." This book prompted us to examine how checklists could revolutionize quality control in our industry. We compared practices across medicine, aerospace, and heavy engineering, identifying weaknesses and potential improvements.

Another story that resonated involved his visit to our transmission factory at Ballabgarh, India. The disarray – oil spills, tangled wires, poor housekeeping – shocked him. He drew a parallel to hospitals, where critically ill patients receive specialized care in controlled environments. This sparked an idea – could we implement a similar tiered approach in our factories, with specialized teams handling complex issues? We even started co-authoring a book exploring this concept, but work pressures eventually side-lined the project.

The Golden Key: A Customer-Centric Masterstroke

One of AB's most impactful ideas was the "Golden Key" program. Traditionally, backhoes took two days to build. However, some machines languished for weeks due to rework and quality issues. AB's vision was to invite customers on a personalized factory tour, allowing them to witness their machine's entire production journey, culminating in a ceremonial key handover.

Initially, I was apprehensive. What customer would want to see their brand-new machine getting repaired? However, this program forced us to prioritize "No Fault Forwarding" (NFF) – ensuring quality at every stage to prevent rework. This customer-centric approach revolutionized our quality mindset.

The Enduring Legacy of Storytelling

Mr. Alan Blake

I was happy to connect back to AB through VS during the course of writing this book and he powerfully reiterated his views as below: "We were acutely aware of the importance of raising JCB India's quality to a global standard if we were to fully realise the opportunity for India to not only lead the market in India but also to take advantage of being an exporter to the many countries that were difficult to service from the UK and Sundar & his Quality team could make it happen. We needed a step change in hearts and minds since continuous improvement from where we were would take too long, our talks were focused on simple thoughts to move minds to a different level of expectation, as I tried to with many talented others in India. The difference I encountered in India compared to other countries and factories that I was visiting was that on subsequent visits the conversations were enhanced and improved, elsewhere they were often left in the wind, and I had to repeat the message."

Yes, We, Indians, actively listen to stories and find that they can help us transform our lives more quickly.

AB's leadership wasn't about pronouncements or directives. He used stories to connect, challenge assumptions, and inspire action. His ability to weave anecdotes into actionable insights left a lasting impact on me, shaping my approach to quality and ultimately, the success of JCB India.

Your Story – Worksheet - 14

Leadership Trait: Memorable (Makes a lasting positive impact on those they lead)

Who:
Write your story:
What are the key learnings?

Chapter 15

Building a Quality Powerhouse

Persistent: Never gives up and overcomes obstacles.

This chapter delves into the importance of persistence in building a high-performing quality team. We'll explore this concept through the story of my collaboration with **Lokesh Pandey** (LP), a phenomenal quality leader who exemplified this trait.

The Missing Piece: Enter LP

As my responsibilities at JCB grew, I realized the need for a strong leader to spearhead the quality department. That's when LP joined us. He possessed a rare combination of skills – analytical thinking, unwavering persistence, a rational approach, and a methodical way of working. My leadership style, on the other hand, was more emotionally driven and focused on identifying the root cause of problems, not just the individuals involved. Despite our contrasting styles, we complemented each other perfectly. The five years we worked together were some of the most rewarding of my career.

A Keen Learner and Propagator

LP was a fast learner. He quickly grasped the concept of field reliability as the bedrock of our quality program and cascaded this philosophy effectively to both supplier and sub-supplier quality. This resulted in the creation of an exceptional quality team – Rahul Misra on field reliability, Sanjay Chaudhury on supplier quality, Sandeep Sabarwal on quality systems, Sanjay Gupta on transmission quality, and Parveen Dawra on fabrication & paint. Under LP's mentorship, this team became the envy of the company. Their focus on a "connected quality story" ultimately translated into a significant increase in JCB's machine resale value, a testament to their dedication.

The team's success was further reflected in the JD Power Survey's PP100 (Problems Per 100) score, which showed a steady improvement between 2005 and 2012, reaching industry benchmarks.

A System for Success

LP's approach to problem-solving was structured and efficient. He categorized all field quality issues into three buckets – Manufacturing, Supplier, and Design – with targeted resolution timelines (30, 60, and 90 days respectively). This simplified the review process across the entire value chain.

He also actively managed supplier behaviour by insisting on advanced notification for any process or inspection system changes. This philosophy – "no surprises" – ensured that any potential negative impact could be assessed and mitigated.

Furthermore, LP established a comprehensive quality architecture with three pillars: Proactive, Control, and Reactive

Quality. He placed a particular emphasis on sub-system reliability, a topic that resonated deeply with me.

Visualizing Quality

One of LP's most impactful innovations was the concept of Quality Command Centres. These large visual boards displayed real-time quality performance data across product, process, and system aspects. They became a ubiquitous sight in JCB's factories and supplier bases, serving as constant reminders of the team's focus on quality.

From Leaks to Leak-Free

An anecdote perfectly illustrates the team's unwavering commitment. When a new cabin design leaked during monsoon season, a service head jokingly suggested offering free umbrellas. This comment deeply impacted the quality team, who saw it as a reflection of a lapse in functional quality. They mobilized swiftly to identify and eliminate the root cause of the leaks. Building on this experience, LP spearheaded a "Leak Free" program focused on eliminating oil leaks in hydraulics, engine, and transmission systems.

Investing in People

LP firmly believed in the power of quality training. He structured a comprehensive program encompassing functional skills, quality tools & techniques, and behavioural aspects. He recognized that while knowledge was important, the right attitude was essential to break the cycle of recurring quality issues.

A Cherished Partnership

Mr. Lokesh Pandey

LP was an invaluable asset to JCB. He exemplified the power of persistence in building a high-performing quality team. Our collaboration remains a highlight of my career, and I consider it a privilege to have worked alongside him. LP's leadership embodied the spirit of persistence – never giving up and constantly overcoming obstacles. LP moved onto Havells India and now leads their Manufacturing Operations as Senior Vice President.

Your Story – Worksheet - 15

Leadership Trait: Persistent (Never gives up and overcomes obstacles)

Who:
Write your story:
What are the key learnings?

Chapter 16

Embracing New Frontiers

Bold: Takes calculated risks and seizes opportunities

This chapter explores the importance of taking calculated risks and seizing opportunities in leadership. We'll see this concept come alive through the story of **Pooja Varshney**, a young engineer who exemplified this trait in a new and challenging role.

Building a New Breed: The Current Product Engineering Team

As my responsibilities at JCB grew, I took on the additional role of managing Current Product Engineering. This team's purpose was to handle engineering changes for released products, freeing up R&D to focus on new innovations. The team would address quality issues, manufacturability concerns, and cost-reduction opportunities, all requiring modifications to existing product designs.

JP Sahu (JP) and Pooja Varshney (Pooja) joined this newly formed team. JP brought experience, but he was still adapting to our work style. Pooja, on the other hand, was a young and ambitious engineer with the potential to become a future leader. With a new function and roles still being defined, expectations were high. Despite the challenges, both JP and Pooja rose to the occasion, exceeding expectations.

A Young Star Emerges

Pooja stood out for her boldness, articulation, and studious nature. Both team members were hands-on, constantly striving to deliver exceptional results and exceeding targets.

One significant challenge we faced was achieving our Year-over-Year (YoY) cost-saving target for Value Analysis/Value Engineering (VA/VE). These targets were set at the machine level (Rs/machine), with no room for error. Monthly financial reviews by the Managing Director (MD) included this critical performance metric.

Leading the Charge

Given the team's youth and inexperience, I initially worried about meeting the target. Typically, seasoned design professionals have a deeper understanding of change requirements and approach them with more confidence. Thankfully, we had the unwavering support of Sameer Das (SD) from R&D. SD's vast experience made him an invaluable resource for our young team. He knew the machines inside and out and readily offered his wisdom and guidance.

However, VA/VE projects were often met with resistance. While finance and purchasing departments loved them, production and quality teams often viewed them with apprehension. These projects often involved process changes, mini design verification and validation exercises, parts inventory control, and a minimum three-month performance monitoring system post-implementation. There were even instances where VA/VE changes were introduced and later withdrawn due to unforeseen issues. This inherent risk made many departments hesitant to cooperate fully.

Bulldozing Through Barriers

This is where Pooja's boldness shone through. She wouldn't take no for an answer. She persistently followed up with everyone involved, relentlessly chasing the entire value chain to ensure project completion. This often required taking calculated risks. Crude prototypes were sometimes necessary to validate concepts before large-scale production decisions could be made.

Thinking Outside the Box

Ms. Pooja Varshney

One example of Pooja's ingenuity involved supplier workshops for idea generation. When tasked with organizing these workshops, both Pooja and JP embraced the challenge. Pooja meticulously planned them, transforming the idea generation process into an exhibition-style event. Suppliers presented parts, subassemblies, and assemblies, allowing internal and external teams to brainstorm while directly visualizing the components within the machine's context. These workshops yielded a wealth of ideas, categorized as immediate, medium-term, and long-term projects. An effort-versus-results matrix helped prioritize initiatives. This innovative approach proved highly successful, enabling us to consistently surpass our cost-saving targets.

Calculated Risks: The Catalyst for Success

In this environment, where navigating complex systems and interpersonal dynamics was crucial, a bold and risk-taking leadership style was essential. Pooja's unwavering determination and willingness to take calculated risks were the driving forces behind the team's success. Her approach serves as a testament to the power of calculated risks and seizing opportunities in achieving leadership excellence.

With these distinct qualities she was able to take responsibility of functional leader in Honda R&D, Mechanical Design Head leading digital transformation in Addverb, an emerging robotics company and currently she is Product head R&D in CNH Industrial.

Your Story – Worksheet - 16

Leadership Trait: Bold (Takes calculated risks and seizes opportunities)

Who:
Write your story:
What are the key learnings?

Chapter 17

A Forceful leader

Competitive: Strives for excellence and motivates others to do the same

This chapter explores the leadership style of **Subir Chowdhury**, a dynamic and energetic leader who significantly impacted JCB India's operations.

Subir: A Forceful Leader

Subir Chowdhury is a highly energetic and inspiring leader. His competitive spirit is infectious, motivating those around him to achieve peak performance. We shared a close friendship, openly discussing workplace challenges and activities. His transparency fostered a trusting environment. Subir's direct communication style leaves no room for misinterpretations about his mood or expectations. A board in his office exemplifies his leadership philosophy: "Are you a player or a spectator?"

Manufacturing Expertise and Strong Network

Subir's leadership of JCB India leveraged his extensive experience from Eicher Motors. He thrived in a collaborative environment, rarely seen alone in his cabin. His frequent walks across the shop floor resembled a "Captain General" inspiring action. These walks often resulted in a flurry of activity as he encouraged continuous improvement suggestions, ensuring everyone had tasks to implement.

The P100 Project: A Collaborative Triumph

Subir spearheaded the ambitious P100 project, aiming for 100 machine production per day. This remarkable feat required a high-performing team meticulously assembled by Subir. The team comprised highly skilled individuals like Gunjan Malhotra (Process Engineering), Navneet Sethi (Supply Chain), Dr. Dheeraj Verma (Health & Safety), Lokesh Pandey (Quality), Subhasish Das Gupta (HR), Sanjay Daftari (Procurement), Sanjay Kathuria (Operations), Michael Chiles (Engine Manufacturing), and myself.

Subir's leadership fostered a competitive environment, driving all team members to strive for excellence. Benchmarking against industry leaders became a core tenet, pushing the team to continuously improve.

The Engine Manufacturing Gamble: A Defining Moment

A significant turning point for JCB India was the decision to manufacture engines in-house at the Ballabgarh factory in 2008. Previously, engines were sourced from external suppliers like Kirloskar. This bold move coincided with stricter emission regulations, adding further pressure. The executive team expressed concerns about potential volume or quality issues impacting market share. Developing a new engine platform required extensive testing, dealer service network preparation, production line stabilization, employee training, and establishing a robust supply chain for castings, machining, and components. The undertaking seemed daunting and fraught with risk. A "Plan B" to continue sourcing engines with upgrades was proposed as a risk mitigation strategy.

Subir, however, believed in the power of a singular focus. His philosophy was that "people who do not plan well, plan for Plan B," suggesting a lack of commitment to Plan A's success. Subir declared "there is no Plan B" for the engine project, emphasizing a "succeed or fail" mentality with "failure not an option." This unwavering focus galvanized the team, leading to the project's successful completion. When driven by a competitive spirit and a relentless pursuit of excellence, success becomes the only option.

This philosophy resonated deeply, and I still have a poster in my cabin that reflects it: "It doesn't matter whether you're the lion or a gazelle – when the sun comes up, you'd better be running."

Subir: A Mentor and Motivator

Mr. Subir Chowdhury

Subir's intense and transparent communication both within and across the teams encouraged a great team work. Everyone was deeply engaged not only to his area but also connected to the larger purpose of the organisation. It was fun to succeed together and keep celebrating the key milestones that we achieved.

The key to our success was continuous talent development and challenging the leaders to grow a strong talent pipeline.

JCB Jaipur is a great milestone, especially on the scale and complexity of the footprint and challenges on achieving the gender diversity on the shop floor, a unique story crafted under his guidance, which is covered under a separate chapter.

Subir is a leader who empowers his team to excel under pressure. His relentless focus on achievement eliminates the concept of "giving up" from his vocabulary. He embodies the leadership trait of "Competitive: Strives for excellence and motivates others to do the same."

Subir's journey continued as he became CEO of JCB India and then moved on to become President of HiTech Gears. Our friendship remains strong, allowing me to seek his guidance whenever needed. He is truly a friend, philosopher, and a great motivator.

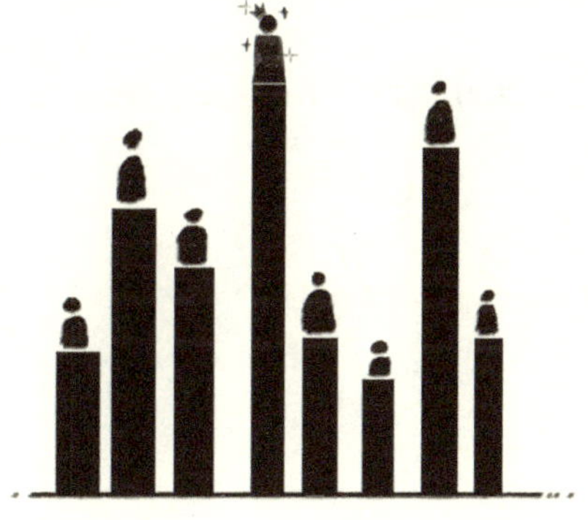

Your Story – Worksheet - 17

Leadership Trait: Competitive (Strives for excellence and motivates others to do the same)

Who:
Write your story:
What are the key learnings?

Chapter 18

Building a Backhoe Giant

Visionary: Sets a clear direction and inspires others to follow

This chapter details the formation of the **Jaipur Leadership Team (JLT)** and their journey in setting up a world-class backhoe factory for JCB in the scorching desert like land of Jaipur.

The JLT: A Symphony of Skills

Mr. Pulkit Garg

The vast, empty landscape with only two porta cabins echoed with the name - JLT. JLT, short for Jaipur Leadership Team, comprised five individuals with distinct expertise:

- **Pulkit Garg**: Leading civil building construction and projects.

Mr. Pradeep Kathuria

- **Pradeep Kathuria**: Overseeing financial matters.
- **Sanjay Kathuria**: Spearheading manufacturing engineering and process planning.
- **Navneet Jaitley**: Managing HR & administration.
- **Rakesh Kumar**: Heading the supply chain and logistics.

This "five-men army" under my leadership embarked on an ambitious mission - to establish one of the world's largest backhoe factories.

Mr. Sanjay Kathuria

Vision: A Collective Dream

I firmly believe that visionary leadership is not a solo act. It's a shared dream, relentlessly pursued by a united group, especially crucial for large-scale greenfield projects. Building a massive factory goes beyond grandeur; it demands meticulous planning for:

- Manufacturing Process: Installing world-class equipment and interconnected machinery for seamless operation.
- Skilled Workforce: Building a team with the right skillset, shared values, and both technical and behavioural expertise.
- Vendor Ecosystem: Establishing a network of reliable suppliers for raw materials, parts, and components.

Mr. Navneet Jaitly

- Financial Prudence: Ensuring a steady cash flow with robust financial controls.

Just like the five fingers on a hand, each department - Civil Projects, Manufacturing Engineering, HR, Purchasing, and Finance - played a vital role. Their combined visionary leadership motivated their teams, turning the vision into reality.

From Barren Land to Bustling Factory: 18 Months of Cohesion (2013-2015)

Mr. Rakesh Kumar

The following 18 months witnessed the JLT's remarkable teamwork. The once barren land transformed step-by-step:

- Building the Infrastructure: From painting fences to planting greenery, the physical structure took shape.
- Building the Workforce: Recruitment drives targeted rural villages and towns, focusing on underprivileged backgrounds, ITI and Diploma holders, and promoting gender diversity. Notably, a large group of women welders were trained and deployed.
- Technological Integration: The team established an IT infrastructure to connect machines and directly feed production data into ERP systems.

- Advanced Automation: Robotic welding cells and Rail Guided Vehicles were planned for heavy material movement.
- Vendor Network: A strong vendor base was established in and around the factory.

"One Team, One Dream" became the guiding slogan, uniting everyone involved - from the initial team to the future workforce. The grand factory inauguration marked the culmination of their collective effort. A unique team-building activity involved creating a giant portrait using handprints as peacock feathers, symbolizing the vibrant diversity of the first 40 employees.

"One Team One Dream" - Inspiring Vision not only created a World Class Facility but brought in a Culture of Excellence, commitment, delivery, cost & governance. This team developed processes which later become bench mark for JCB group. Every employee become brand ambassador for Jaipur Plant within JCB group. Employees at all levels engaged & participated in societal activities in villages and schools around the factory. All employees engaged in those initial days have a lifelong impression in their life & the power of "One team One Dream" - inspiring vision. The HR team comprised key individuals, including Sanjeev Pareek, Nageshwar Lakhawat, Amit Tyagi, Monideepa Roy.

Fully Integrated Civil Building & Services ensured Zero discharge facility, completely integrated utilities including pipeline delivery of operating consumables for the weld shop, Green & Sustainable Footprint ensured integrated solar electrification with Integrated Landscape & Interiors. The interesting part is we even had even hailstorm during construction in a barren land including flash floods which tested the 5-acre large pond created for rainwater harvesting for the entire facility. The project team comprised key individuals, including Annamalai Ramanathan, Santosh Saxena, Itish Jayawant, Praveen Arora, and Saket Vats.

Manufacturing operations were planned to be flexible, optimized and with No Fault Forward Footprint along with IT enabled Man / Machine / Material Interfaces with built in Lean Supply Chain & Logistics Management. The project team comprised key individuals, including Vishal Awasthi & Neeti Kaushik.

Since heavy structural fabrication is the nature of the factory operations, the concept of "Live & Breathe Welding: "Everyone is a Welder" was implemented. Ingrained Diversity & Emotive Connect Initiatives were undertaken and Experiential Training towards JCB Production System was implemented.

Financial compliance and budget control are essential activities in any large project. It's important that they act not as stumbling blocks but as enablers while maintaining necessary controls. This role was ably handled by Pradeep Kathuria and his team, which included Ajay Malhotra, Abhishek Agrawal, Sandeep Chouhan, and Bhagwati Sharma.

This chapter exemplifies how a group of visionary leaders, with their distinct skills and a shared dream, can turn a desolate landscape into a thriving industrial hub.

Picture source: https://www.kalpariartandmind.com/projects.html

Your Story – Worksheet - 18

Leadership Trait: Visionary (Sets a clear direction and inspires others to follow)

Who:
Write your story:
What are the key learnings?

Chapter 19

From Shop Floor to Director

Driven: Possesses a relentless pursuit of goals

This chapter explores the concept of "Driven," a crucial leadership trait exemplified by **Seshadri Raman** (Sesh), the son of a former colleague, SSR. We'll witness how Sesh's relentless pursuit of goals propelled him from a graduate engineer to a Director of Operations.

Restless and Relentless: The Hallmarks of Drive

Having drive is not merely a desire for achievement. It's a potent combination of restlessness and relentless pursuit of goals. The self-driven individual excels at charting a course and navigating efficiently towards the desired outcome.

Sesh embodies this trait perfectly. He thrives on challenges and embraces ambiguity, readily taking ownership of unclear tasks. He then meticulously carves a path, guiding his team along a well-defined course.

Burning Bright: Sesh's Early Days at JCB

The early days at JCB were a baptism by fire for Sesh. Unbound by traditional working hours, he poured at least 20 hours a day into his work. A new factory was taking shape in JCB Jaipur, and Sesh shouldered the responsibility of leading a team of fresh recruits. They had a daunting task - mastering production processes and readying complex equipment for production, all within a tight timeframe.

Mr. Seshadri Raman

The environment was demanding. Steel cutting, bending, and welding are no easy feats. To foster a culture of understanding, we established a welding training school. Everyone, from office staff to senior leaders, donned the welding gun and experienced the artistry and challenges of this vital skill. Young and energetic college graduates like Mukesh Pareta, Lokender Hada, Hemant Yogi, Gajender Singh, Mahavir Prasad, Sanjib Shatapathy, Akshay Chouhan, and Rajesh Gaur joined the team. After a brief training program, they transitioned straight into the job with enthusiasm and dedication.

Sesh, however, possessed a natural affinity for welding. He quickly absorbed the intricacies, his talent evident in the way he could diagnose welding current and gas flow consistency from a distance based on the sound and visual cues. This technical proficiency, coupled with his relentless drive, made him a powerful force on the shop floor.

Red-Eyed and Relentless: The Price of Progress

Greenfield projects are rarely smooth sailing, and ours was no exception. Challenges were abundant, but Sesh tackled them with unwavering diligence. Some mistook his rapid rise for favouritism, considering his prior connection to me and his father.

However, the reality was far different. I nicknamed him my "red-eyed boy" - a testament to the countless hours he spent in the welding shop. Despite necessary PPE, the welding flames took their toll, often leaving his eyes bloodshot and swollen.I worried about his well-being, fearing fatigue would hinder his progress.

Despite his junior status compared to the seasoned JLT members, Sesh's insights were invaluable. His inclusion in leadership meetings ensured a crucial ground-up perspective, keeping the team in touch with the realities of the shop floor.

Sesh's relentless pursuit of goals, evident in his early days at JCB, proved to be a defining leadership trait. This drive would propel him to greater heights, leading him to follow me to Pricol and eventually securing his current position as Director of Operations at DHL.

eka ya

Your Story – Worksheet - 19

Leadership Trait: Driven (Possesses a relentless pursuit of goals)

Who:
Write your story:
What are the key learnings?

Chapter 20

Defying the Myth: Strong Women

Strong: Demonstrates resilience, confidence, and decisiveness

This chapter celebrates the remarkable women who shattered stereotypes and thrived as leaders in the male-dominated world of factories. Each displayed a powerful collective trait - **Strength**. This strength manifested as resilience in the face of challenges, unwavering confidence, and decisive action.

Monideepa Roy: Architect of a Diverse Workforce

Ms. Monideepa Roy

Monideepa Roy, the first leader on our team, spearheaded HR, particularly recruitment and training. Our goal was to recruit young talent from rural ITI and Diploma institutes. Monideepa's ingenuity shone through in her custom-designed dexterity testing kits. These kits mimicked welding operations, assessing hand-eye coordination and steady movement - crucial skills for the job.

Beyond technical skills, she understood the importance of addressing societal concerns. Monideepa conducted parent meetings, alleviating anxieties about their daughters working in a factory environment. She also played a pivotal role in achieving our ambitious target of 30% female representation on the shop floor.

Setting up a training facility - both theoretical and practical - in a temporary porta cabin amidst a vast, empty landscape presented a unique challenge. Monideepa tackled it head-on, ensuring a well-rounded learning experience for the recruits.

The cherry on top? She championed the first 20 recruits' three-month intensive training program in the UK. Imagine the transition - from rural India to a completely new environment, requiring adjustments to basic living habits. Monideepa's leadership went beyond professional guidance; she fostered emotional engagement, creating a sense of belonging for these young women.

The Symphony Conductor: Anjali Fredrick

Ms. Anjali Fredrick

Anjali Fredrick, another powerhouse, single-handedly managed my office. She was the central nervous system, overseeing various activities and ensuring seamless coordination. Her meticulous work ethic made her the go-to person for everyone. Data accuracy was paramount, and Anjali's dedication ensured every piece of information reported was the "single point of truth."

She excelled at project management, keeping everyone on track with meeting cadences, following up on commitments, and ensuring smooth collaboration across departments. Anjali even instituted daily site progress photography, creating a valuable visual record for remote senior leaders. In a potentially chaotic environment, Anjali's strength and bold leadership ensured a smooth workflow.

Neha Rathi: The Master of Project Management

Ms. Neha Rathi

Neha Rathi, with her rich automotive project management experience from Daimler, swiftly integrated into the team. She brought order to the project by implementing detailed project management worksheets. These captured activity timelines, dependencies, buffer management strategies, cost overrun control, and quality progress tracking.

Imagine the complexity - multiple activities happening concurrently. Neha's structured approach provided much-needed clarity. Through a comprehensive company-level dashboard, and further breakdowns to functional and individual levels, she ensured everyone had a clear view of progress. Her headstrong personality and talent commanded respect from both seniors and peers, enabling her to navigate the complex environment effectively.

Neeti Kaushik: A Pioneer in Robotics

Ms. Neeti Kaushik

Neeti Kaushik, initially a graduate engineer, quickly rose to the role of Process Engineer. Her expertise in robotics was invaluable. As the first woman leader to travel to our other JCB facilities and robotic cell suppliers in Austria, Neeti played a key role in the introduction and testing of robotic cells for the factory.

Her core work entailed manufacturing layout planning which extended to developing technical and commercial bid packages for equipment suppliers, coordinating timelines and deliveries, overseeing equipment installation and commissioning, and ensuring production and quality targets were met. Neeti even went above and beyond, volunteering as a night shift works manager. This role allowed her to monitor production and ensure the safety of our female workforce on the factory floor.

Neeti's tenacity and resilience were on full display during the robotic trials. Her decisiveness in tackling complex problems was instrumental in keeping the project on schedule.

Ms. Poonam Rana

Poonam Rana: The CSR Champion and Project Leader

Poonam Rana joined the team to spearhead CSR (Corporate Social Responsibility) initiatives and external engagement.This role demanded strong leadership qualities, as she interacted with stakeholders beyond the factory walls.

Poonam designed innovative mechanisms for employee participation in social causes. She fostered a sense of community by ensuring the children and faculty of adopted schools felt like part of the JCB family. Poonam later transitioned to project management roles, playing a key part in new product introductions.

Kanika Gupta: From Campus Leader to Shop Floor Champion

Recruitment isn't just about selecting candidates; sometimes, it's about recognizing potential. During campus interviews, we often miss out on talented student leaders. Fortunately, we didn't make that mistake with Kanika Gupta. While she wasn't formally part of the recruitment process, our team noticed her strong leadership qualities during her role as a student coordinator for industries at MNIT Jaipur.

Ms. Kanika Gupta

Hired for the shop floor production team, Kanika quickly rose to the challenge. She adeptly managed shifts, providing control and guidance to her team. As a pivotal figure, she ensured production planning and inventory management ran smoothly.

These young women, all relatively inexperienced at the outset, demonstrated remarkable strength - a combination of resilience, confidence, and decisiveness. These qualities propelled them to success not just in India, but across the globe. Monideepa now thrives as a senior talent acquisition professional in Australia. Anjali manages a team at Bharat Forge. Neha has risen to the position of Director at Slam Out Loud. Neeti utilizes her expertise as a Business Strategist for a Southeast Asia Start-up. Poonam leverages her project management skills at Philips. And Kanika drives revenue and operations as a Director – Self Operated Business at Oyo.

Their stories are a testament to the power of defying stereotypes. By fostering a culture that embraced diversity and empowered women, we witnessed the emergence of exceptional leaders who left their mark on JCB and beyond.

"The first cohort of female diploma engineers to specialise in welding skills included Jyoti Lakhesar, Jyoti Sen, Diksha Sharma, Puneeta Singh, and Jasu Devi. Among them, Jasu Devi, often hailed as a 'Lady Robot,' was the subject of a captivating video titled "Passion & Progress of Jasu Devi," which remains accessible on YouTube. Over the years, these pioneering women have excelled as engineers and managers, forging successful careers in their respective fields."

Your Story – Worksheet - 20

Leadership Trait: Strong (Demonstrates resilience, confidence, and decisiveness)

Who:
Write your story:
What are the key learnings?

Chapter 21

Leading with Caution

Wary: Exercises caution and considers all possibilities

Between 2015 and 2018, I found myself back in southern town Coimbatore, leading Pricol, a major auto-component company, as its President. We supplied electronic clusters and mechanical pumps to some of India's biggest two-wheeler manufacturers, with factories spread across the country. One of our most crucial and rapidly growing markets was the Northern region, managed by the highly experienced **Tarun Tandon**.

Tarun's leadership style could be best described as **wary**: he exercised extreme caution and considered every possible scenario before taking action. This meticulous approach was the cornerstone of his success. Before making any commitment, be it to management or a customer, he would meticulously research the situation, evaluate potential risks, and essentially do his complete homework. This careful nature translated into an almost perfect success rate for his projects.

The High-Stakes Game of Auto Components

The auto-component business is a fiercely competitive landscape. Major Japanese technology companies and other players dominate the market. With giants like Maruti, Honda, and Toyota leading the four-wheeler segment, and Honda, Suzuki, Yamaha, and Kawasaki at the forefront of the two-wheeler segment, competition for technology and market share is fierce.

Furthermore, product lifecycles are short, necessitating rapid design changes. Since the bill of materials is often transparent, margins are constantly under pressure. India, being the world's largest two-wheeler market at 20 million vehicles annually, demands high production volumes. Quality expectations are nothing short of world-class, with parts-per-million (PPM) rejection rates being surpassed by stringent parts-per-billion (PPB) flawless supply requirements.

Leading with 360-Degree Awareness

Given these demanding conditions, factory heads need to be incredibly cautious on all fronts to defend and grow their business. Tarun possessed a remarkable 360-degree leadership perception, keeping him and his team constantly on alert. Even a single rejection from the customer triggered immediate action. His quality control team would identify the root cause and initiate corrective actions upstream, while he would personally connect with the customer to explain the issue and assure them of preventative measures.

Supplier delays were handled with similar urgency. His staff would travel to the supplier's premises, even on weekends, to ensure a smooth flow of materials and prevent production line stoppages. He personally monitored absenteeism to guarantee uninterrupted production. This focus on "Run at Rate," a concept crucial for high-volume production lines, was further bolstered by a robust quality control system including Poka-Yoke (mistake-proofing), set-up approvals, ongoing line inspections, and pre-dispatch product audits.

The Importance of Getting it Right the First Time

Tarun was particularly involved in New Product Introduction (NPI) activities, even though a separate team managed them. He understood that once a product was accepted, the customer would be closely monitoring its implementation and ensuring real-time adherence to QCD (Quality, Cost, Delivery) parameters. Any mistakes during introduction could have a cascading effect, jeopardizing customer launches, halting their production lines, and potentially leading to significant revenue and profitability losses in the long run if competitors capitalized on the opportunity. This is why he was always wary and insisted on getting it Right First Time (RFT).

Proactive Monitoring for a Healthy Supply Chain

Similarly, Tarun and his team were constantly vigilant about potential field failures. If any problem arose with a running product due to variations in supplied parts or overlooked quality control, the entire value chain could be severely disrupted. In the automotive industry, product recalls are a major concern, and Tarun was meticulous in ensuring Pricol's components never caused brand image damage to the Original Equipment Manufacturers (OEMs) they supplied. Real-time performance monitoring and proactive responses formed the core of his strategy to maintain control of the situation.

He also managed to add a new plant with minimum overhead costs and extended managed support from the existing plant and within a stipulated time frame meeting both capacity expansion and customer needs.

Preparedness is Key

Mr. Tarun Tandon

As the saying goes, "It's better to be safe than sorry." Tarun's leadership style, characterized by wariness and meticulous planning, perfectly embodies this proverb. He considered every possibility and ensured his team was always ready to respond. In my career, he stands out as a prime example of how anticipation and proactive problem-solving are essential for success in the high-pressure world of auto components. Tarun continues to lead Pricol with the same unwavering commitment, keeping the company at the forefront of the industry.

Your Story – Worksheet - 21

Leadership Trait: Wary (Exercises caution and considers all possibilities)

Who:
Write your story:
What are the key learnings?

Chapter 22

The Steady Hand

Authentic: Leads with genuine self-belief and transparency

In the world of leadership, authenticity is a powerful quality. It refers to leading with genuine self-belief and transparency, acting in alignment with your values, and fostering trust within your team. This quality becomes even more crucial when navigating uncharted territory, as I experienced during my time at Wipro.

In early 2018, I joined Wipro to head a brand-new business vertical – Automation Solutions. This was an exciting but daunting prospect. We were a small team, venturing into a new market with limited resources and an uncertain path to success. However, having **Pratik Kumar** as our leader instilled a sense of confidence in all of us.

Pratik: A Beacon of Calm and Clarity

I had the privilege of interacting with Pratik earlier, during my tenure with JCB and he as CEO of Wipro Infrastructure. Even then, he struck me as a leader who embodied a sense of calmness and clarity. He possessed a clear vision for the future, yet remained grounded and approachable.

This authenticity proved invaluable when leading our new venture. Pratik established a culture of transparency through meticulous weekly reviews. He actively listened to understand our ideas and plans, fostering a collaborative environment. This open communication allowed us, a small team, to leverage resources effectively and build a roadmap for success.

Overcoming Challenges with an Authentic Leader

Starting a new business within a large organization can be unsettling, especially for seasoned professionals like myself. However, Pratik's authenticity helped alleviate these anxieties. He fostered a culture of trust and empowered us to take calculated risks. This allowed us to openly discuss and address challenges, paving the way for setting audacious goals (BHAGs) for our new venture.

The Indian automation market presented a unique opportunity. While demand was high, particularly in the automotive industry, there was a lack of established players offering customized turnkey solutions. Pratik recognized this gap and provided the support needed to capitalize on it. We adopted a strategic mix of organic and inorganic growth strategies to accelerate our presence in this market.

The Importance of Trust in Acquisitions

Rapid growth through partnerships and mergers and acquisitions (M&A) involves complex negotiations and due diligence processes. However, the most critical factor in securing a successful deal is often the human element – trust.

Pratik understood this well. During the final stages of negotiations, he would personally step in to meet with the promoters of target companies. His genuine demeanour, charisma, and proven track record served as a powerful assurance, convincing them that their businesses were in good hands.

Leading with Confidence Through Growth

Companies experiencing high growth rates face unique challenges. Investments in people and infrastructure need to be made in anticipation of future demand. Pratik's leadership played a vital role in navigating this phase. His clear communication, self-belief, and transparent approach instilled confidence in both the board and the senior leadership team. He empowered us to make crucial decisions and secure funding to support our ambitious goals.

The Power of Authenticity

Mr. Pratik Kumar

Pratik's leadership style is a testament to the power of authenticity. He consistently delivered on his promises, fostering a culture of trust and open communication. He empowered his team to dream big, provided clear direction, and established a robust system for monitoring progress. In my experience, Pratik exemplifies authentic leadership at its best, guiding us with a steady hand as we ventured into uncharted territory.

Your Story – Worksheet - 22

Leadership Trait: Authentic (Leads with genuine self-belief and transparency)

Who:
Write your story:
What are the key learnings?

Chapter 23

The Power of Experimentation

Xeniel: Embraces new ideas and perspectives

There's a certain magic that happens when you bring together a group of curious minds, all eager to push boundaries and rewrite the rules. It's this very energy that fuelled the early days of our Automation Vertical, and it all started with **Jyotirmoy Ray**, my first hire.

Jyotir: A Force of Creative Disruption

Jyotir wasn't just another engineer; he was a walking innovation lab. His thirst for knowledge and his relentless pursuit of "what-ifs" made him the perfect fit for a team tasked with exploring uncharted territories. Jyotir embodies the leadership trait of being a Xeniel: someone who not only embraces new ideas but actively seeks them out.

This innate curiosity manifested in Jyotir's early work on Human Sensory Intelligence (HSI) based automation. It was a radical concept – integrating all five human senses into technology. We spent countless hours brainstorming possibilities, from using touch sensors to improve casting and forging processes to replicating the subtle nuances of smell and taste for tasks like tea brewing and rice quality checks. While HSI remains a work in progress, the project perfectly exemplifies Jyotir's approach – exploring the fringes of what's possible.

Beyond the Textbook: Experimentation Takes Centre Stage

Jyotir's influence extended beyond theoretical explorations. He was a passionate advocate for practical applications. One such example was his work with Cobots (collaborative robots). Jyotir, along with a team of Graduate Engineer Trainees (GETs), built a coffee-making Cobot for an exhibition. Visitors could order their drink through a tablet, and the robot would flawlessly prepare it. This playful demonstration showcased the potential of Cobots in unexpected environments.

Similar innovative spirit went into projects like 3D bin picking with machine vision and a damage assessment robot for rental cars. The latter was an autonomous mobile robot (AMR) equipped with a camera pole, allowing for contactless damage inspection while maintaining safety protocols. These projects, though diverse, shared a common thread – a willingness to experiment and challenge the status quo.

Innovation in the Face of Crisis: A Xeniel Response to Covid-19

The global pandemic threw everything into disarray. Factories shut down, projects stalled, and the world held its breath. But even amidst the chaos, Jyotir's team refused to be side-lined.

They channelled their creative energy into developing solutions to combat the pandemic's effects.

They designed a walking sanitization channel for public spaces, an AMR for delivering essential supplies in Covid wards, and even an automated hand sanitizer dispenser with temperature checks and facial recognition attendance recording. These projects were a testament to the power of a Xeniel mindset. Jyotir and his team didn't wait for solutions to fall into their laps; they actively sought them out, working tirelessly to bring their ideas to life.

The Rise of the Xeniel Leader

Jyotir's leadership style reflects a growing trend – the rise of the Xeniel leader. This leadership approach, where embracing new ideas is paramount, is rapidly becoming the new normal across generations and industries. We are already witnessing a shift in traditional companies, with CXOs (Chief Experience Officers) emerging in their mid-thirties, bringing fresh perspectives and innovative approaches to leadership roles.

As we stand on the brink of a new era in technology and business, it is clear the future belongs to the Xeniels – those who dare to dream big, experiment relentlessly, and turn the impossible into reality. These leaders aren't defined by their age or generation, but by their mindset and approach to innovation.

The Xeniel leader, exemplified by Jyotir, thrives on challenging conventions and pushing boundaries. They create environments where curiosity is not just encouraged but celebrated, where failure is viewed as a steppingstone to success, and where the impossible is constantly being redefined.

In this rapidly evolving landscape, organizations that cultivate and embrace Xeniel leadership will find themselves at the forefront of innovation. These leaders, with their unique blend of creativity, adaptability, and forward-thinking, are poised to navigate the complexities of our ever-changing world and drive meaningful change.

Mr. Jyotirmoy Ray

Jyotir's story serves as a powerful reminder that innovation thrives in environments where new ideas are welcomed, experimentation is encouraged, and the status quo is constantly questioned. As we look to the future, it's clear that the Xeniel approach to leadership will be instrumental in shaping the next wave of technological advancements and business transformations.

Your Story – Worksheet - 23

Leadership Trait: Xeniel (Embraces new ideas and perspectives)

Who:
Write your story:
What are the key learnings?

Chapter 24
The Steadfast Captain

Loyal: Commands trust and dedication through unwavering support

The Balancing Act of Finance

The finance department of any large organization is often seen as traditional, yet its leadership demands a distinct style rooted in proven success. This leadership can be described as steadfast—commanding trust and loyalty through unwavering support.

Imagine leading a ship across a vast ocean; the ship represents the company, and its financial resources are your charts and compass. As the captain, you must be both an enabler—providing the resources necessary for growth—and a guardian—ensuring responsible spending and compliance with regulations. It's a delicate balance, managing risks, capital allocation, cash flow, and legal frameworks. This is where a financial leader like **Shripad Ramanathan** truly excels.

Predictability Breeds Trust

Shripad exemplifies the essence of clear, dependable leadership. His approach is rooted in establishing predictable and consistent expectations. Standardized reporting formats, well-defined metrics, and transparent communication are the pillars of his leadership style. Confusion and misinterpretation have no place in his realm.

He follows a methodical routine: regular reviews supported by pre-structured data that highlight early signs of issues. His emphasis on open communication extends to frequent one-on-one meetings with senior management, ensuring everyone remains aligned and surprises are kept at bay.

Beyond Routine: Embracing Innovation

Yet, Shripad is not limited to routines. When confronted with critical decisions—such as mergers, acquisitions, or other strategic financial moves—he skilfully shifts gears. In these moments, he demonstrates his ability to think beyond the familiar, embracing new methods, complex financial models, and innovative assessment techniques.

His approach to these high-stakes situations is comprehensive. By analysing a range of outcomes—both optimistic and conservative—Shripad ensures a balanced evaluation of every opportunity. This strategic adaptability, paired with his innovative mindset, is built on a foundation of trust. Having earned the confidence of his team and superiors through his reliability, he is able to introduce novel solutions that are readily accepted.

Loyalty: The Cornerstone of Ethical Leadership

In any large multinational organization, core values like ethics and integrity are fundamental to maintaining the company's reputation. A loyal financial leader embodies these values, demonstrating unshakeable dedication to ethical practices.

Shripad is a prime example of this ideal. His steadfast loyalty extends beyond maintaining the financial health of the company—it underpins his commitment to ethical leadership.

Mr. Shripad Ramanathan

Shripad's unwavering support has guided the finance function in numerous new business ventures. His accomplishments, such as being recognized as one of the "40 Under 40 CFOs," underscore his value as a leader. His story proves that loyalty in financial leadership goes beyond stability; it is about driving the organization forward with integrity, innovation, and the highest ethical standards.

Your Story – Worksheet - 24

Leadership Trait: Loyal (Commands trust and dedication through unwavering support)

Who:
Write your story:
What are the key learnings?

Chapter 25

From Humble Beginnings to Global Automation Leader

Yearning: Sets high goals and strives for continuous improvement

Building a Dream, One Repeatable Solution at a Time

Today, we celebrate the success stories of Indian techies returning home to serve the nation. But what about pioneers who paved the way decades ago? In 1990, long before the current wave, two technocrats, Mangesh Kale and Ranjit Date, returned from the US and defied the odds. In Pune, India, they embarked on a daring venture: a robotics automation company named PARI (Precision Automation and Robotics India).

Their journey is a testament to a powerful leadership trait: **Yearning**, which manifests as setting high goals and striving for continuous improvement. Over three decades, PARI blossomed into one of India's finest engineering enterprises, serving a wide range of industries with complete turnkey automation solutions. By 2021, when Wipro acquired PARI, it was already a global leader with factories in the USA and a strong international presence.

Sadly, we lost Mangesh Kale along the way. However, the team he meticulously groomed continues to make his dreams a reality on the world stage. **Dr. Ranjit Date**, who now leads Wipro PARI, embodies the essence of Yearning.

The "Repeatable, Scalable & Sustainable" Mantra

One of Ranjit's guiding principles, a mantra that stuck with me, is the pursuit of **"Repeatable, Scalable & Sustainable"** business solutions. Throughout their journey, like in any entrepreneurial venture, Ranjit and his core team—comprising Govind Oza, Amit Joshi, Rophin Paul, Atul Patil, Ashish Datey, Sagar Deshmukh, Khanderao Shinde, Vishvajit Dabak, Avinash Adige, and Vineet Joshi—experimented with various automation solutions across diverse sectors. They tackled projects ranging from the nuclear industry to steel bar bundling and even bank locker systems.

However, over time, Ranjit recognized the key to significant organizational growth: **"Doing more of what we are good at."** He prioritized solutions that could be replicated across projects and customers. Repeatability translates to predictability in execution, reduced time and resource consumption, streamlined project management, and a higher chance of meeting customer timelines and expectations.

Scaling Solutions and Building Customer Trust

The next step in Ranjit's philosophy is **scalability**. He envisions taking the same solution to different factories across the globe, both for a single customer and across multiple clients. Scalability involves stitching together reputable technologies into market-specific turnkey solutions.

The Power of Continuous Improvement

Now, this pursuit of excellence wouldn't be complete without **continuous improvement (CI)**. As Ranjit himself says, CI acts as a "peg" that prevents backsliding and ensures progress on the path to achieving high goals. This philosophy translates into building strong structures and systems within the organization.

Building a Culture of Continuous Improvement

Dr. Ranjit Date

As the company grows, the structure needs to adapt as well. The challenge lies in striking a balance: avoiding excessive silos while fostering deeper skillsets in employees. A growing organization must address both the horizontal breadth and vertical depth of its market segments and technological deployments.

When it comes to systems, the key is not to parachute them in from outside. Effective systems are carefully developed over time, with enough flexibility to adapt and evolve alongside the organization. Ranjit's grasp of both structures and systems has been instrumental in fostering CI as a habit and core company culture.

Yearning: The Fuel for Exponential Growth

Setting high goals and striving for continuous improvement – these are the hallmarks of the leadership trait we call Yearning. This is the very force that propels an organization towards an exponential growth trajectory. Witnessing this firsthand as Co-CEOs of Wipro PARI has been a truly remarkable experience.

Your Story – Worksheet - 25

Leadership Trait: Yearning (Sets high goals and strives for continuous improvement)

Who:
Write your story:
What are the key learnings?

Chapter 26

The Power of Passion

Zealous: Possesses a strong passion for the cause or vision

From Quality Champion to Growth Catalyst

This final chapter delves into a fundamental leadership trait: **Zeal**. It's the unwavering passion you possess for a cause or vision, the fire that keeps you motivated and inspires those around you. Let's explore how this trait has manifested throughout my own 35-year career journey.

Igniting a Passion for Quality

My story begins with a spark – a fascination with quality philosophy, tools, and techniques. In 1991, this spark ignited into a flame when I was sponsored to learn Taguchi methods at the Indian Statistical Institute. Imagine being mentored by giants like Dr. Genichi Taguchi, the pioneer of Loss Function Analysis and Design of Experiments, and Dr. C. R. Rao, a recipient of the International Prize in Statistics!

This experience fuelled my zeal for quality. I actively implemented these concepts, leading to successful deployments across numerous projects. This passion propelled me towards

TQM (Total Quality Management) roles, further enriching my knowledge.

Continuous Improvement: A Contagious Drive

My zeal for quality wasn't confined to personal learning. I actively fostered a culture of continuous improvement. As a member of the American Society for Quality (ASQ), I pursued certifications like CQE (Certified Quality Engineer), CQM (Certified Quality Manager), and CSBB (Certified Six Sigma Black Belt). This journey didn't stop there. I delved into lead auditor courses for ISO standards and product reliability.

In various organizations, "Product Reliability" became our mission. We utilized Reliasoft Weibull analysis to break down warranty data, ultimately enhancing product performance beyond the warranty period. This not only strengthened brand loyalty but also established a competitive edge in resale value. This is the power of zeal – it translates passion into tangible results.

Strengths, Not Weaknesses: Building on What's Strong

Early in my career, Gallup's Strengths Finder exercise left a lasting impression. I firmly believe that leaders are unique individuals. They rise to the occasion based on a combination of their key strengths. Of course, everyone possesses weaknesses too. However, the traditional leadership development approach often focuses on "fixing" these weaknesses.

My approach differs. Unless a weakness is absolutely detrimental to the organization, I believe in leveraging strengths. Through tools like Strengths Finder and 360-degree feedback, I identify individuals' key strengths and then focus on amplifying them. It's far easier to build upon existing strengths than to struggle with improving the weaknesses. Seeing my subordinates flourish using this approach has been incredibly rewarding.

The Fire of Growth

Mr. Sundararaman

I've always held the firm belief that organizations need continuous profitable growth. Stagnation is a recipe for decline. Think of growth as oxygen for a company. A stagnant top line or a CAGR (Compound Annual Growth Rate) below market average is a red flag.

This is where a leader's **zeal for growth** comes in. Senior leadership teams need a healthy dose of restlessness when profitable growth isn't on track. The ability to identify and implement strategic actions for organic and inorganic growth (both within current markets and through expansion) is crucial.

Your Story – Worksheet - 26

Leadership Trait: Zealous (Possesses a strong passion for the cause or vision)

Who:
Write your story:
What are the key learnings?

Recap

Here's a revisit of the A-Z leadership traits that we explored in the book:

1. **A - Authentic:** Leads with genuine self-belief and transparency.
2. **B - Bold:** Takes calculated risks and seizes opportunities.
3. **C - Competitive:** Strives for excellence and motivates others to do the same.
4. **D - Driven:** Possesses a relentless pursuit of goals.
5. **E - Energized:** Infuses the team with enthusiasm and motivation.
6. **F - Fearless:** Makes tough decisions and isn't afraid of challenges.
7. **G - Grateful:** Appreciates contributions and fosters a positive environment.
8. **H - Honest:** Builds trust with open communication and integrity.
9. **I - Inspirational:** Motivates and empowers others to achieve their best.
10. **J - Just:** Makes fair decisions and treats everyone with respect.
11. **K - Knowledgeable:** Possesses expertise and fosters a culture of learning.
12. **L - Loyal:** Commands trust and dedication through unwavering support.
13. **M - Memorable:** Makes a lasting positive impact on those they lead.

14. **N - Networker:** Builds strong relationships and fosters collaboration.
15. **O - Obsessive:** Ensures accuracy and high standards.
16. **P - Persistent:** Never gives up and overcomes obstacles.
17. **Q - Qualified:** Possesses the skills and experience to lead effectively.
18. **R - Responsible:** Takes ownership of actions and decisions.
19. **S - Strong:** Demonstrates resilience, confidence, and decisiveness.
20. **T - Tactful:** Delivers feedback and navigates difficult situations with diplomacy.
21. **U - Unwavering:** Holds firm to their values and convictions.
22. **V - Visionary:** Sets a clear direction and inspires others to follow.
23. **W - Wary:** Exercises caution and considers all possibilities.
24. **X - Xeniel:** Embraces new ideas and perspectives.
25. **Y - Yearning:** Sets high goals and strives for continuous improvement.
26. **Z - Zealous:** Possesses a strong passion for the cause or vision.

Epilogue

"Leadership is not just one quality, but rather a blend of many qualities; and while no one individual possesses all of the needed talents that go into leadership, each man can develop a combination to make him a leader."

– Vince Lombardi (who is considered by many to be among the greatest American football coaches)

There's no magic bullet – successful leaders don't subscribe to a single style. Throughout this A-Z exploration, we've seen a rich tapestry of leadership traits, each contributing to triumphs. Observe the leaders around you, analyse what resonates, and adapt your approach. Remember, the beautiful paradox of leadership is that the coexistence of diverse styles is what makes the journey so dynamic and ultimately, successful.

Credits

This book, *EmBossed Imprints: A-Z Leadership Traits,* has been a labour of love and collaboration. It would not have been possible without the contributions of several remarkable individuals, to whom I extend my deepest gratitude:

All the Leaders

Whose leadership traits are showcased through anecdotes and examples. I am grateful to each of you for reviewing your respective content, granting permission for publication, and providing your photos. Your stories are at the heart of this book.

Mr. Jyotirmoy Ray

Jyotirmoy Ray, Scientist, Wipro Research, Bengaluru For his invaluable help in reviewing the book, suggesting changes, and making thoughtful modifications that significantly enriched its content.

Ms. Akshaya Bharadwaj

Akshaya Bharadwaj, Final Year Engineering Student, Mukesh Patel School of Technology Management and Engineering, Mumbai For her artistic contributions by providing beautiful paintings and sketches that breathe life into the pages of this book.

Dr. Divya Kumawat, Psychologist and Art Therapist, Kalpari Art & Mind, Bengaluru For her creativity in designing and executing the handprint motifs and for the captivating picture featured in one of the chapters.

Dr. Divya Kumawat

Priya Darshana, Publishing Manager, Notion Press For her patience and diligence in offering editorial support, crafting the cover design, shaping the interior layout, and accommodating iterative changes with unwavering dedication.

Ms. Priya Darshana

Without the support, creativity, and expertise of all those mentioned above, the creation of *EmBossed Imprints* would have been immensely challenging. Thank you for making this journey a meaningful and successful endeavour.

Afterword

"Stories are the single most powerful tool in a leader's toolkit."

– Howard Gardner (who is an American cognitive psychologist and author, best known for his theory of multiple intelligences)

A-Z Leadership Traits:

The foundation laid.

Now, get ready to build the

A-Z Leadership Toolbox!

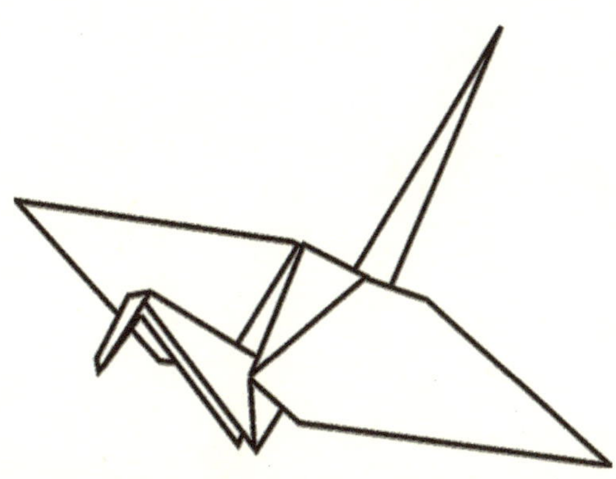

www.ingramcontent.com/pod-product-compliance
Lightning Source LLC
LaVergne TN
LVHW090927150826
845672LV00006B/1426

* 9 7 9 8 8 9 6 3 2 2 1 0 8 *